The Nazareth Jesus Knew

I am the light of the world.
Whoever follows me will never walk in darkness
but will have the light of life. —*John 8:12*

THE NAZARETH JESUS KNEW

Thanks to the Bible Society of Israel for their generous cooperation with this book.

Our special thanks to Sherry Herschend for making this publication possible.

Text: Joel Kauffmann
Design: Merrill Miller
Editing: S. David Garber, Keith Graber Miller
Photography: D. Michael Hostetler. Also: Mark Goodman, LeRoy Troyer, Joel Kauffmann, Grace Abdo, Merrill Miller
Illustrations and Maps: J. Robert Teringo, Elizabeth Swindle, Merrill Miller
Nazareth Village Program Consultants: Kenneth E. Bailey, Th.D.; Dr. Nakhle Bishara; Joel Kauffmann; Stephen Pfann, Ph.D.; Mark Goodman; Ross Joseph Voss; Cary Summers.

The historical and archaeological research for Nazareth Village was conducted by the University of the Holy Land under the direction of Stephen Pfann, Ph.D., utilizing a strict methodology. The archaeological excavations were carried out under the license of the UHL's Center for the Study of Early Christianity (http://www.uhl.ac/) and directed by Ross Voss, M.Th.S., and Dr. Pfann. All site survey and archaeological work was conducted with the proper licensing and procedural requirements as established by the Israel Antiquities Authority.

Methodology: UHL's research for Nazareth Village was based upon the most up-to-date resources in areas of archaeology, ancient literary sources, and socio-ethnographic sources. These sources, and the conclusions drawn from them, were individually evaluated according to a unique rating-scale of certainty.

Rating the Sources and Conclusions: (A) certain, no doubt; (B) probable, little doubt; (C) plausible, possible, some room for doubt; (D) hypothetical, an educated guess.

The results of the research have been archived and formed into reports upon which the construction of Nazareth Village, its farm, and its contents have been based. As new evidence from these sources will become available, the conclusions in the archive and the constructions on the land may be re-evaluated and updated accordingly.

Thanks are due to the UHL research team and staff: Vered Hillel, M.A.; Claire Pfann, M.A.; Yehudah Rapuano, M.A.; Elizabeth Adams; William Broughton, M.A.; Steven Cox, M.A.; Rami Fellemon, M.A.; Erika Miyake; Yoshie Nakai, M.Th.S.; Edwin Rattai, M.A.; Donald Tweedie Jr., Ph.D.; Ross Voss, M.Th.S.; and Sherry Whetstone.

And special thanks to the international team of experts who advised us and reviewed our research reports. Synagogue: Prof. Israel Levine, Prof. Eric Meyers, Prof. Ehud Netzer, Prof. James Strange. Houses and town structure: Fr. Eugenio Alliata, Prof. Anne Killebrew, Dr. Yizhar Hirschfeld, Prof. Vassilios Tzaferis, Prof. Yoram Tsafrir. Olive press and winepress: Dr. Rafael Frankel, Mr. Yehoshua Drey. Farm: Dr. Shimon Gibson, Dr. Rafael Frankel. Material culture: Yehudah Rapuano, M.A.; Dr. Eitan Ayalon; Fr. Jean Baptiste Humbert; Guy Stiebel, M.A. Social Setting: Prof. Israel Levine, Dr. Kenneth Campbell, Prof. Sean Freyne, Prof. James Charlesworth, Prof. William Horbury. Conservation and reconstruction: Mark Goodman, M.A.; Dr. Giora Solar.

Our gratitude to Dr. Kenneth E. Bailey, whose lifelong passion for illuminating the first-century meaning of Jesus' parables has profoundly shaped the program at Nazareth Village and key sections of this publication.

Nazareth Village is grateful to all who gave generously of their time, talents, prayer, and resources to help restore the last surviving first-century Nazareth farm and to lovingly re-create the village Jesus called home. In these pages, you'll witness the handiwork of the many volunteers, board members, staff, advisers, and supporters who have made Nazareth Village possible. But our greatest reward will be that you see more clearly and compellingly the central reason for all our efforts: Jesus of Nazareth.

CONTENTS

JOURNEY BACK TO THE TURNING POINT IN TIME

Nazareth Village, a historic site in the Holy Land, is dedicated to rediscovering the Nazareth that Jesus knew. You are invited to journey with us back 2000 years, back to the turning point in time.

WELCOME TO FIRST CENTURY NAZARETH VILLAGE

From Sherry Herschend,
Miracle of Nazareth International Foundation

Nathanael asked, "Can anything good come from Nazareth?" Philip answered, "Come and see."
—*John 1:46*

So what amazing thing did Philip want Nathanael to see?

Jesus of Nazareth! A man revered by Jews as a rabbi, by Muslims as a prophet, and by billions of Christians worldwide like myself as Savior and Lord.

Of course, if Nathanael had known the answer, he would have needed no prompting from Philip. And now that you know the answer, I invite you also to come and see.

Nazareth Village, set in the heart of Nazareth, Israel, is a re-creation of ancient Nazareth that adjoins an authentic first-century farm. It was created through the cooperation of Holy Land Christians with the international Christian community.

Nazareth Village is a labor of love with Christ at the center. And we want to share it with the whole world. So in the pages that follow, we—the founders, planners, scholars, staff, and supporters of Nazareth Village—offer a sampling of what we have discovered on this exciting journey.

Come and see!

Nazareth Village is a labor of love with Christ at the center. And we want to share it with the whole world. —Sherry Herschend

Sherry Herschend, here working with Dr. Bishara, is one of the many who made Nazareth Village and this book possible by responding to the invitation "Come and see."

From Dr. Nakhle Bishara,
Nazareth Village Board of Directors

There is a deep desire on the part of all who come to Nazareth to see Jesus. But for centuries, all they could see was dusty stones. That is why I proposed a place where visitors could see those ancient stones come to life and witness the vineyards and olive trees Jesus used to teach spiritual truth.

I am excited that this dream is now a reality. I believe Nazareth Village will be a gift of peace to the world, and also to those of us who live, work, and worship in a land torn by conflict.

From Prof. Stephen Pfann,
Center for the Study of Early Christianity

Our institution has been engaged for two decades in a quest to reconstruct a village representing the life setting of Jesus' ministry based upon the most up-to-date resources. It has been our great joy to be able to join in this vision to re-create ancient Nazareth with other fine institutions, inspired individuals, and indeed with the citizens of Nazareth themselves.

RICK DIAMOND

Aerial view of Nazareth Hospital overlooking Nazareth Village being built.

From EMMS Nazareth

The Nazareth Hospital was founded in 1861 by the Edinburgh, Scotland, Medical Missionary Society (now called EMMS Nazareth). Since its earliest days, the hospital has served the community and provided healing in the name of Christ to all who needed it, irrespective of race, colour or creed. It is a place of peace and reconciliation for all peoples.

We are delighted, through the sharing of our land, to be involved with Nazareth Village, serving the Lord Jesus Christ and building and developing his kingdom on earth, particularly among the people of the Middle East. We invite you to learn more about Nazareth Village and the Nazareth Hospital and how we are working in harmony to promote hope and healing in the heart of the Holy Land.

From President Jimmy & Rosalynn Carter, Honorary Trustees of Nazareth Village

Jesus' life and teaching will no longer be bound to words, but will come alive for all who take part in the Parable Walk and this re-creation of first-century Nazareth. Welcome.

For my thoughts are not your thoughts, nor are your ways my ways, says the Lord. —*Isaiah 55:8*

WHY NAZARETH?

Of all the times and places throughout human history, why was first-century Nazareth the ideal location for Jesus to call home? How did Nazareth help prepare Jesus for his work? The following facts offer some tantalizing clues to contemplate.

1. Strategic importance. For the first 5000 years of recorded history, whoever controlled the 40-kilometer-wide (25-mile) strip of land between the Mediterranean and the Jordan River on which Nazareth sits had the upper hand in world politics. Many of the decisive battles in history were fought here.

2. Roman roads. Roads built by the Roman Empire connected Nazareth and Galilee to the rest of the world, and in time they would transport Jesus' good news to the far corners of the empire. Five decades before the birth of Jesus, these roads did not exist.

3. A place of shelter. Though Jesus lived in turbulent times, Nazareth, surrounded by a ring of hills, offered shelter and solitude, making it an ideal place to nurture body and spirit.

4. Diversity of people. The location of Nazareth in Galilee placed Jesus in a setting where he could experience people from a wide variety of cultures and backgrounds.

5. Diversity of setting. Jesus likely spent time working in the fields surrounding Nazareth and building homes in the nearby trade city of Sepphoris. This allowed him to draw on both the rural and urban experience for examples in his teaching.

6. Herodian dynasty. The power and corruption of the Herods, who ruled the Holy Land through the first century, provided an ideal backdrop for contrasting human kingdoms, built on fear and military might, with God's kingdom, rooted in love and reconciliation.

7. Humility and simplicity. Nazareth was a humble place, filled with hardworking villagers who had to struggle against rocky soil and heavy taxes to survive. Jesus drew on this natural setting for parables emphasizing God's grace, mercy, and compassion.

Remains of a Roman road at Sepphoris.

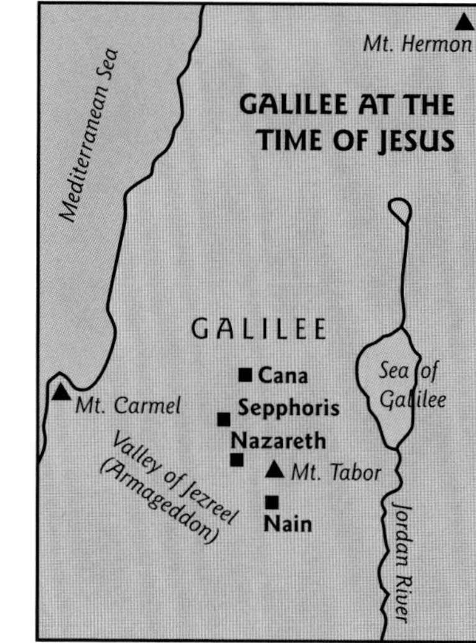

Creating a living presentation of the life, times, and teachings of Jesus of Nazareth for all the world.

WHY RE-CREATE FIRST-CENTURY NAZARETH?

1. Very little exists of ancient Nazareth. What remains has provided the foundation for scholars and specialists to piece together a picture of Jesus' hometown. The result, Nazareth Village, gives pilgrims a compelling reason to come to Nazareth and a place to walk as Jesus walked.

2. The geographical and cultural nuances of Jesus' teaching are often crucial for understanding his full meaning. At Nazareth Village, visitors can experience how a first-century audience heard and was impacted by Jesus' words.

3. Pilgrims to the Holy Land see the dead stones of ancient ruins, but often miss the living stones of Jesus' legacy: the believers who have lived, worked, and worshipped here since Pentecost. Nazareth, home to many gracious and hospitable Christians, provides an ideal setting for interaction.

Nazareth Village was built and is run by a partnership between Christians in the Middle East and the international church.

Top: Nazareth Village maintains its homes and fields in the manner of the first century, creating a continuous laboratory that is producing exciting new discoveries into the life and teachings of Jesus.

Above: Along with pilgrims from around the world, thousands of children from across the Holy Land visit Nazareth Village each year.

Nazareth Village features a carefully researched re-creation of Jesus' hometown. The surrounding terraces and farm features did exist in Jesus' day. In fact, Nazareth Village preserves the last remaining fields worked by Jesus' friends, family, and fellow villagers.

RE-CREATING FIRST-CENTURY NAZARETH

Step One. Begin with an authentic, first-century farm located less than 500 meters (540 yards) from the site of ancient Nazareth, which lies under the Basilica of the Annunciation and a modern market.

Extensive archaeological excavations carried out by the University of the Holy Land's Center for the Study of Early Christianity show that Nazareth Village land was being quarried and farmed at the time of Jesus. The ancient agricultural features that were discovered include three watchtowers, a winepress, stone quarries, farm terraces, and a spring-fed irrigation system. The south-facing hillside offered plenty of sun, drainage, and calcium-rich soil, all ideal for growing grapes and making wine, a main industry of first-century Galilee.

Pottery sherds located on the land are like fingerprints to a detective. They provide a reliable way for archaeologists to piece together the puzzle of what happened on this land, and when.

Irrigation System

Watchtowers

Basilica of the Annunciation

Quarries

Winepress

Terraces

Pottery Sherds

Step Two. Explore similar sites and conduct historical, anthropological, and archaeological research.

Nazareth Village, partnered with the University of the Holy Land, conducted field surveys of 20 past and current excavations and spent two years combing ancient texts. The result was a growing body of evidence regarding the farming and building techniques of Jewish agricultural villages in the Early Roman Period.

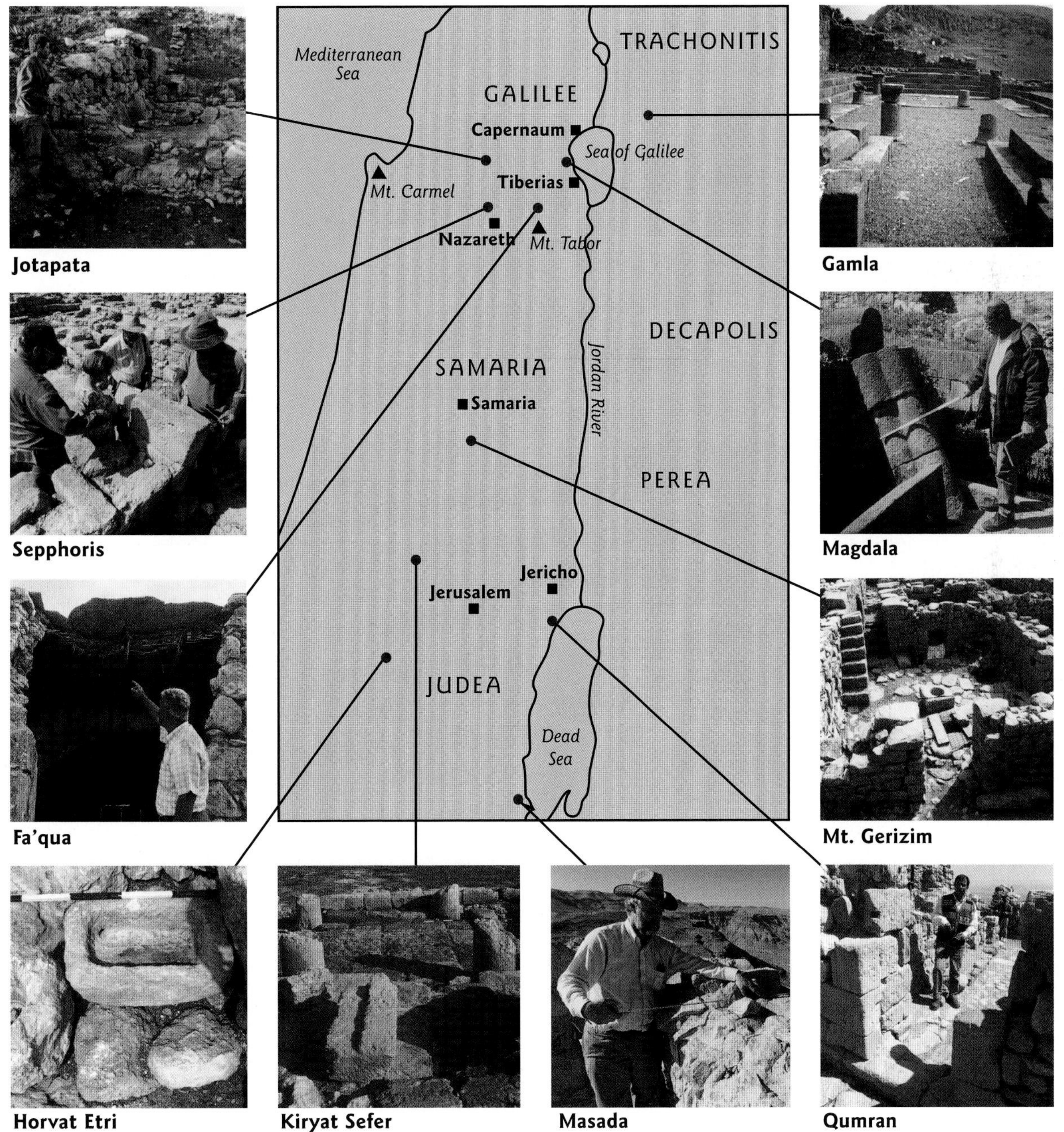

Jotapata

Sepphoris

Fa'qua

Horvat Etri

Kiryat Sefer

Masada

Qumran

Mt. Gerizim

Magdala

Gamla

Step Three. Building on historical research and field surveys, restore the terraces to their original condition and construct a village that re-creates first-century Nazareth as accurately as possible, using identical materials and building methods. Pictured here is the construction of the Nazareth Village synagogue. More information is available on the Nazareth Village Web site (NazarethVillage.com).

Ancient Masada (left) provides a rare, complete example of the columns for a first-century synagogue. These are measured precisely, then replicas are quarried in Jenin from a fine white limestone, matching stone used to carve the ancient columns found under the Basilica of the Annunciation.

While first-century synagogues were each unique, scholars agree that they had several common features, including inner walls surrounded by benches and a central space defined by a colonnade.

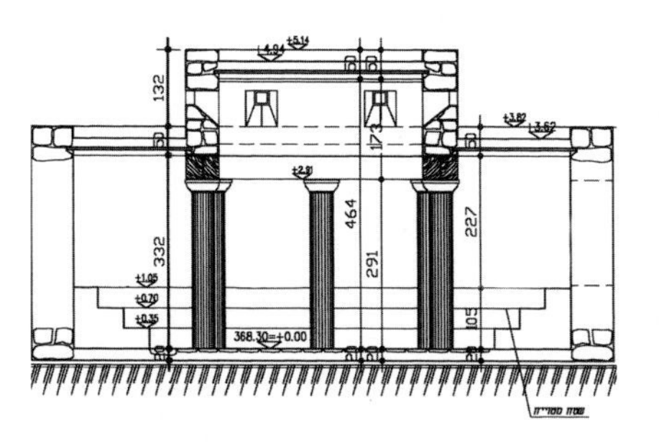

The stacked columns stand ready to be crowned with the capitals. Benches will be carved from the natural bedrock.

Because no first-century synagogues remain standing in the Holy Land, the higher one builds the less certain one can be about how it looked. Some archaeologists believe the roof remained open, but it's more likely that the heart-shaped corner columns supported a clerestory roof.

Heavy, squared beams are positioned across the colonnade. They have to support the cross timbers of the lower roof as well as the stone wall of the upper (clerestory) roof. The carving of the benches begins.

Heavy stones are set and wedged with smaller stones (chinks). A mortar of earth, straw, and lime fills the void in the walls. Quarry cuts are integrated into the walls.

When completed, the interior of the synagogue is plastered with a two-layered technique. The base coat is lime and sand mixed with wood ash to improve adhesion and prevent cracks. The second layer includes a fine mixture of white lime and quarry sand. Along with the white interior, the clerestory windows provide ample light and ventilation, making this a pleasant place for worship and public gatherings.

SEVEN COMMON MISCONCEPTIONS ABOUT JESUS AND NAZARETH

1. Jesus spent only his childhood in Nazareth.

In fact, Jesus spent his childhood, youth, and most of his adult years in Nazareth. Jesus' only years away from Nazareth were his first few, when he was exiled in Egypt, and the last three, when he was teaching and healing throughout Galilee.

2. Nazareth was a small, isolated village.

Nazareth was neither small nor isolated. It lay on the outskirts of Sepphoris, the largest city in Galilee, and also its capital during most of Jesus' years in Nazareth. Sepphoris, a thriving trade center, would have exposed Jesus to people from many backgrounds, and to the complexity of urban life.

3. Herod, the ruler of Galilee, was a deranged and dangerous man.

This description fits Herod the Great, who ruled Judea and Galilee when Jesus was born. During Jesus' Nazareth years, the ruler of Galilee was Herod the Great's son Herod Antipas, who, though ambitious and crafty (Luke 13:32), generally ruled in a civil manner. Herod Antipas's bad reputation came from his act of beheading John the Baptist (Matthew 14), which haunted him the rest of his life. Beyond that tragic incident and the later war against his former father-in-law, Aretas IV, king of Nabatea, there is no record of Herod Antipas putting anyone to death.

4. Jesus was a carpenter.

In this day before specialization and in a land where trees were scarce and rocks plentiful, it is almost certain that Jesus would have been a builder who worked with both stone and wood. One reason Joseph may have brought his family back to Nazareth is that there was abundant work rebuilding Sepphoris, which had been completely destroyed in 4 BC (see pages 24-27).

5. Jesus was a simple, untutored man.

The fact that Jesus was called "Teacher" and "Rabbi" suggests that he had earned this respect through training and a sophisticated understanding of Scripture. In Jesus' day, students were not always sent off to special schools to become religious leaders; some studied in their own village. Rabbis were expected also to carry on an occupation such as carpentry so they could support their families and better relate Scripture to daily life (see page 49).

6. Jesus grew up in an all-Jewish region.

Though Nazareth was Jewish, Galilee was also home to many Gentiles, which often created conflict and resentment. Jesus fueled this tension by suggesting that God's good news was not just for one people, but for all (see pages 49-51 and Matthew 4:15).

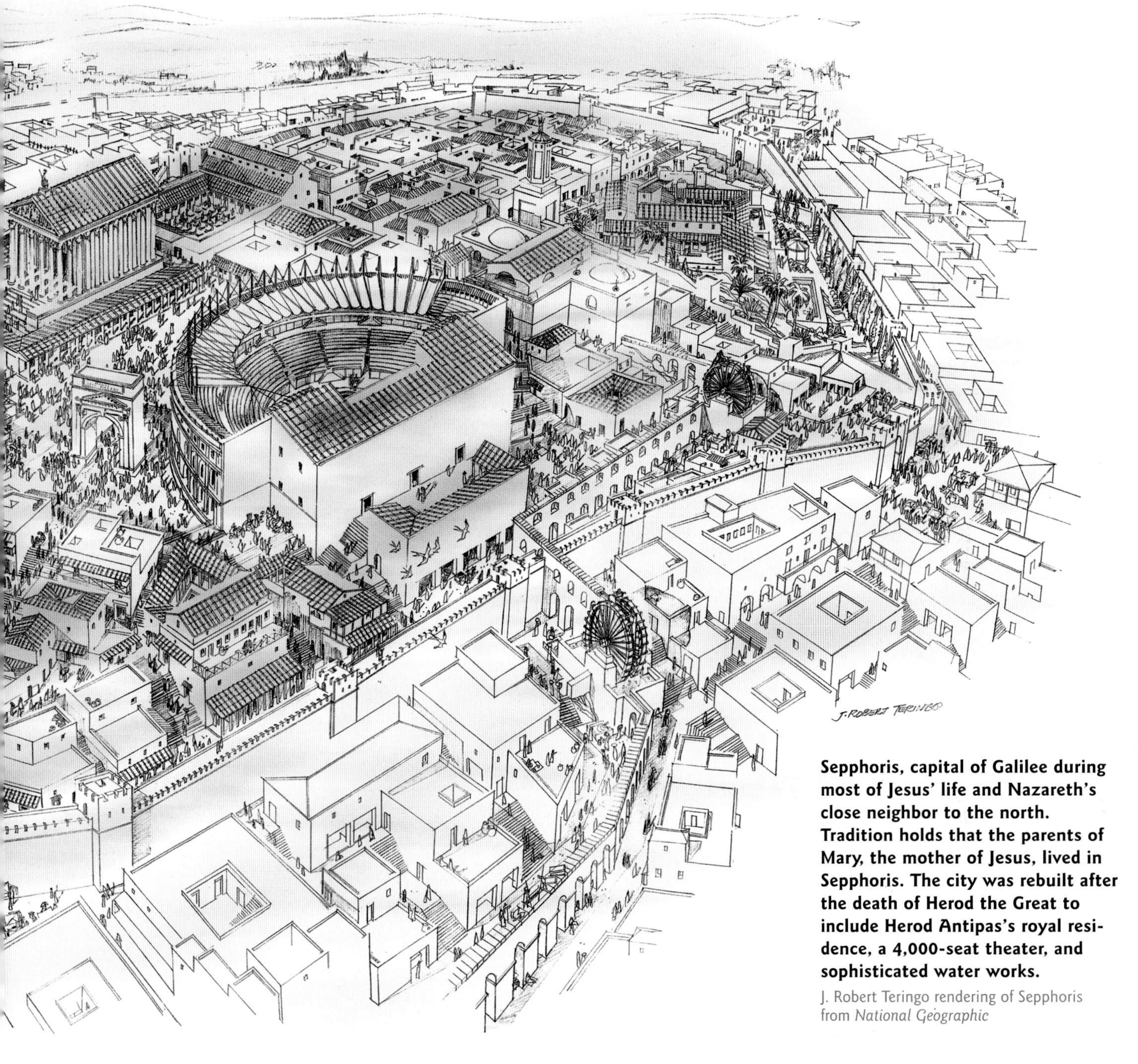

Sepphoris, capital of Galilee during most of Jesus' life and Nazareth's close neighbor to the north. Tradition holds that the parents of Mary, the mother of Jesus, lived in Sepphoris. The city was rebuilt after the death of Herod the Great to include Herod Antipas's royal residence, a 4,000-seat theater, and sophisticated water works.

J. Robert Teringo rendering of Sepphoris from *National Geographic*

7. Jesus was "a good man."

While the poor and powerless viewed Jesus as "a good man" (John 7:12), many of the powerful came to see Jesus as a troublemaker. Socializing with women and sinners and calling for love of enemies (an unfamiliar and unwelcome concept in that time) were just several ways Jesus overturned the rules of first-century society and became a threat to civic and religious order. Ironically, the first attempt on Jesus' life came at the hands of his Nazareth friends and neighbors (see pages 50-51). By the standards of first-century Galilee, then, Jesus was either the Messiah or "a bad man."

THE TURNING POINT IN TIME

Emperor Tiberius

40-37 BC Herodian dynasty begins as Rome names Herod the Great King of Judea. It takes him three years to put down rebellions and secure his rule.

20 Birth of Herod the Great's youngest son, Herod Antipas.

6/4 Birth of Jesus in Bethlehem. Also, of Jesus' cousin John the Baptist. Joseph, Mary, and the child Jesus flee to Egypt to escape Herod the Great. The birth of Jesus, considered as the turning point in time, actually takes place several years earlier due to a later error in calculation. The intended date was AD 1 (there is no year 0).

4 An eclipse of the moon (recorded by Flavius Josephus) took place just before the death of Herod the Great. This event has been used to help determine the birth and chronology of Jesus Christ.

Death of Herod the Great in Jerusalem.

Varus, governor of Syria, puts down a revolt at Sepphoris and destroys the city, which neighbors Nazareth.

Herod Antipas, studying at Rome, is appointed ruler of Galilee at age 16. His title is "Tetrarch": he rules one-fourth of the kingdom. The remainder of the kingdom is awarded to brothers Archelaus and Philip after a contentious court battle in Rome.

AD 7/9 Jesus, 12 years old, debates with religious leaders at the temple in Jerusalem. This is the last record of Joseph in Scripture.

14 Reign of Roman Emperor Tiberius begins.

23 As a tribute to Emperor Tiberius, Herod Antipas founds Tiberias on the Sea of Galilee to be his new capital. Building began years earlier, but was slowed by the discovery of Jewish burial sites.

50 45 40 35 30 25 20 15 10 5 1 5 10 15 20

JESUS' TIME IN NAZARETH (3 B

3 Herod Antipas returns from Rome, selects Sepphoris as his new capital, and begins to rebuild it as his showcase. He gives it the official name of Diocaesarea in honor of Caesar Augustus, though this name is not commonly used. Building continues until AD 10 and perhaps beyond.

Herod Antipas marries the daughter of Aretas IV, King of Nabatea (kingdom southeast of Palestine), to reward him for his help in crushing the rebellion that followed the death of Herod the Great.

Joseph, Mary, and Jesus return to Nazareth. They take care to avoid Archelaus, who has begun ruling Judea with a cruelty resembling that of his father.

Herod the Great ordering the massacre of the innocents.

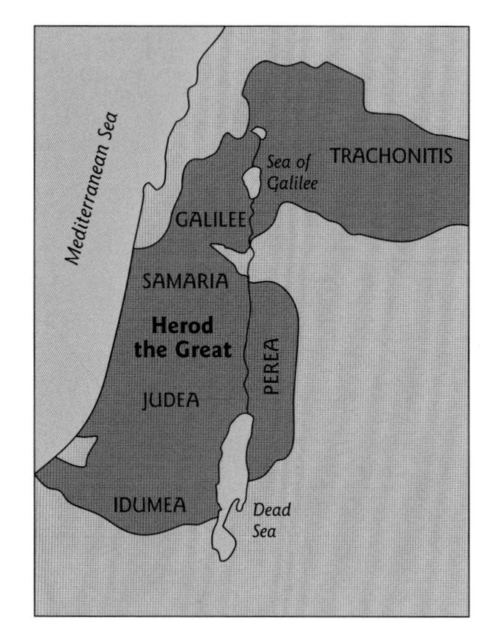

The Holy Land during the reign of Herod the Great.

These dates should be considered as estimates. Many are based on the careful research and convincing chronology provided by Harold W. Hoehner in his 1972 Cambridge University Press publication, *Herod Antipas*.

26 Pontius Pilate begins as procurator/prefect of Judea. Antipas objects to Pilate's harsh treatment of Galileans who visit Jerusalem. The two leaders remain at odds until the crucifixion of Jesus (Luke 23:12).

29 Herod Antipas, now nearly 50, divorces his wife and marries Herodias, his niece by one brother, and wife of his half brother. The ambitious Herodias believes Herod Antipas should rule over all the kingdom, as did his father, Herod the Great, as King of the Jews.

Jesus leaves Nazareth to begin his ministry. John the Baptist baptizes him in the Jordan River.

31 John the Baptist beheaded by Herod Antipas at the request of Herodias at their fortress at Machaerus near the Dead Sea. Herod Antipas believes thereafter that Jesus is the ghost of John the Baptist (Mark 6:16).

33 Jesus arrested and tried in Jerusalem. Jesus and Herod Antipas meet for the first and only time, even though their lives have intertwined for three decades. Jesus crucified under a sign "King of the Jews" and resurrected on the third day.

36 King Aretas defeats Herod Antipas in battle as revenge for the humiliation of his daughter. Many consider this as divine punishment for his murder of John the Baptist.

Herod Antipas with step-daughter Salome.

39 Herod Antipas's quest to be king ends when he is tricked out of his title by Herodias's brother Agrippa I. Herodias chooses to accompany Herod Antipas into exile, even though Agrippa offers her clemency.

47 Paul begins his missionary journeys.

92 End of Herodian dynasty with the death of Agrippa II. Christian faith continues to spread like wildfire and just over two centuries later is openly embraced by the Roman Empire of Constantine the Great.

30 35 40 45 50 55 60 65 70 75 80 85 90 95

30

30 Herodias moves with her young daughter, Salome, to Herod Antipas's royal palace at Tiberias overlooking the Sea of Galilee.

John the Baptist begins to preach relentlessly against the marriage of Herodias to Herod Antipas, which violates Mosaic law. Herodias fears that John's opposition threatens her husband's ambitions.

Following the arrest of John the Baptist (Mark 1:14), Jesus centers his ministry in Capernaum, just up the Galilean shore from Tiberias and visible from Herod's palace. While Antipas continues to have difficulty attracting residents to Tiberias, crowds flock to Capernaum to hear Jesus speak and perform miracles.

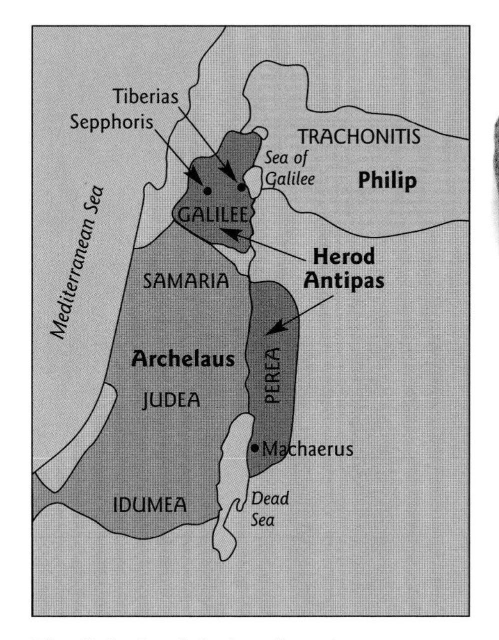

The Holy Land during the reign of Herod Antipas.

A rare bronze coin minted by Herod Antipas at Tiberias, possibly in the year of Jesus' crucifixion and resurrection. The Greek letters ΛΖ refer to the 37th year of Herod Antipas's reign over Galilee, or AD 32/33. The inscription on the circumference of the coin reads ΗΡΩΔΟΥ ΤΕΤΡΑΡΧΟΥ, Herod the Tetrarch. The inscription on the back reads TIBEPIAC, Tiberias. The symbols are distinctly Jewish. These coins were intended solely for the local needs of Antipas's tetrarchy, which included Nazareth.

NAZARETH AND GALILEE AT THE TIME OF JESUS

In Jesus' day, population centers were divided into three categories: villages, towns, or cities. Over the years, the most common theory argued that Nazareth was the smallest of these: a village with a population of a few hundred at most. The Gospels refer to Nazareth as a town, but some scholars argue that the evangelists exaggerated the size of Nazareth because of its importance as Jesus' home.

First-century Nazareth likely was a town with a population between 400 and 1,200. Here are some of the clues: (1) The inhabited area was perhaps as large as 160 dunams (40 acres), and in Jesus' day people lived in close quarters. (2) Nazareth could support its own synagogue. And (3) Nazareth was ideally located close to the capital city of Sepphoris, which offered ample opportunities for work and trade.

Another intriguing though less scientific clue: Jesus based many of his parables on Nazareth. One parable tells of ten bridesmaids who waited at night for a wedding. Five of them forgot to bring extra oil for their lamps and had to go buy more. While they were away, the groom arrived, the doors were closed, and the five bridesmaids missed the wedding. A village would not have a place to buy oil, and it is too small for anyone to be gone long enough to miss the arrival of the groom. But if Nazareth were larger, as a town, both would be possible.

The primary language of Nazareth was Aramaic, which was closely related to Hebrew.

Some Numbers for First-Century Nazareth and Its Surroundings

25-30,000	Population of the city of Sepphoris
200,000	Population of Galilee
240	Cities, towns, and villages in Galilee (Josephus notes that 15 of these were large enough to have fortified walls)
800 m/2625 ft.	North-South length of Nazareth (half mile)
200 m/657 ft.	East-West width of Nazareth (eighth of a mile)
600 m/1950 ft.	Elevation of Nazareth above Sea of Galilee
380 m/1250 ft.	Elevation of Nazareth above sea (ocean) level
488 m /1600 ft.	Elevation of hills surrounding Nazareth (above sea level)

Average Temperatures for Each Month
(highs about 6°C /10°F above the average):

C / F		C / F	
11°/52°	January	27°/80°	July
12°/54°	February	27°/80°	August
14°/58°	March	25°/77°	September
18°/64°	April	22°/72°	October
21°/70°	May	17°/63°	November
24°/76°	June	13°/56°	December

253	Average number of days above 21°C/70°F
1	Average number of days below 0°C/32°F
19°C/67°F	Average temperature for year
63.5/25	Inches/centimeters of annual rainfall
33	Degrees latitude (aligned with modern cities of Savannah, Georgia; Casablanca, Morocco; Shanghai, China)
35	Degrees longitude (aligned with Moscow, Russia; Nairobi, Kenya)

Distances from Nazareth

	Kilometers	Miles	Travel Time (then)
Sepphoris	5.6	3.5	1 hour
Capernaum	32	20	1 day
Sea of Galilee	24	15	1 day
Mediterranean	27	17	1 day
Jerusalem	104	65	5-7 days
Rome	3,000	1,860	55-73 days

Travelers could cover 17 Roman miles (15-16 modern miles/25 kilometers) by land each day, depending on the terrain. Jerusalem required more time because the direct route through Samaria was difficult and dangerous, and the route along the Jordan River longer. The sailing time to Rome is figured for westward. The return trip could generally be done more quickly.

The educated also would have learned Greek. The population was Jewish, descended from the house of David. The surrounding Galilee was home to many Gentiles, including Romans, Egyptians, Phoenicians, and Greeks. Neighboring Sepphoris was a trade city frequented by people from every corner of the world.

Judeans and Galileans were often critical of each other. Judeans criticized Galileans for their "crude" dialect and for being less strict in religious matters. Galileans criticized Judeans for placing more value on money than honor. Galileans were fiercely independent. "All revolts begin in Galilee" was a familiar first-century saying. This reputation and experience led to Judeans and Romans distrusting Galileans.

Isaiah prophesies that the Messiah will be "a shoot" that springs from the house of Jesse (11:1). Matthew builds on this by writing that Jesus resided in Nazareth, home to descendants of Jesse, so that what was spoken by the prophets would be fulfilled (2:23).

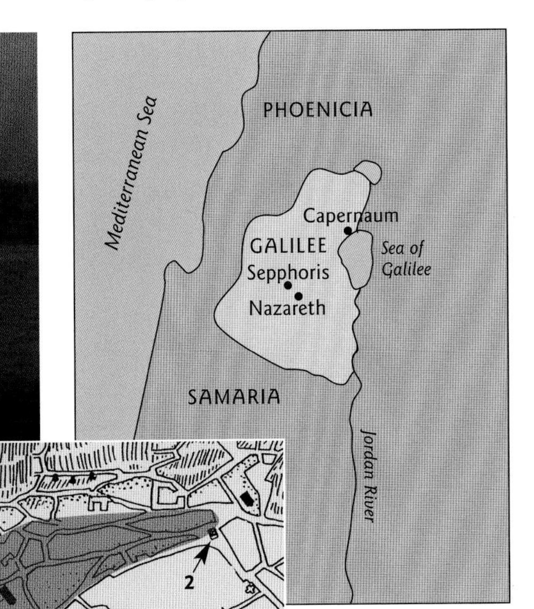

Galilee in Jesus' day was small, measuring only about 1,943 square kilometers (750 square miles). It ran about 48 kilometers (30 miles) north to south and 40 kilometers (25 miles) west to east. First-century Galilee bordered Samaria on the south, Phoenicia on the west and north, and the Jordan River on the east.

Almond shape of ancient Nazareth at the time of Jesus. Mary's house is at the far left (1), Mary's Well at the far right (2).

Nazareth likely derives from the Hebrew word *netser*, which means "a shoot" or "to blossom." The town has been called the Flower of Galilee because it sits in a high, hollow plateau surrounded by a ring of rounded hills that resemble the petals of a rose.

For every mile Jesus walked from the Sea of Galilee to Nazareth, he had to climb 130 feet. For every kilometer traveled, the climb was 25 meters. Most of this climbing took place at the beginning and end of the journey.

THE TOWN JESUS KNEW

When traveling through the Holy Land today, one of the first things visitors notice is that houses never stand alone. The same was true for first-century towns and villages like Nazareth.

Everyone, including farmers and shepherds, lived together in close-knit community. Homes were clustered tightly together, partly for security and friendship, and partly to preserve land for farming.

Trades

Farming was the primary occupation in Nazareth. But merchants such as potters, weavers, and blacksmiths also plied their trades. We know there were at least two builders: Joseph and Jesus. Because Nazareth is close to Sepphoris, which was rebuilt as the capital of Galilee beginning in 3 BC, Nazareth likely served as home for other builders who commuted to this thriving city for work. They preferred living in this comparatively quiet and religiously observant town.

Given the size of Nazareth, there was likely no market where food and wares were sold. The market at Sepphoris would have provided far more lucrative opportunities. Nazareth craftsmen likely plied their trades and sold their products outside their doorways.

Water and News Source

We also know that Nazareth had at least one well or spring, located at its northern and highest end, along the main road into town. The location of the settlement was almost certainly chosen because of this well, and the town depended on it for survival.

The well was also a gathering place where neighbors and friends exchanged greetings and the news of the day. Now known as Mary's Well, it has become the world's most famous spring of water because of its association with the Annunciation (pages 46-47).

Left: For hillside settlements such as Nazareth, the donkey served as the first village planner. Donkeys had an instinct for finding the easiest route up a steep hill. The earliest homes were built along this path, allowing for a street wide enough to accommodate a donkey loaded with baskets. Eventually, the main street through town let two such burdened donkeys pass each other.

The Lost Coin, a village-based parable Jesus tells in Luke 15:8-10, is one his neighbors could identify with. "What woman having ten silver coins, if she loses one of them, does not light a lamp, sweep the house, and search carefully until she finds it? When she has found it, she calls together her friends and neighbors, saying, 'Rejoice with me, for I have found the coin that I had lost.' Just so, I tell you, there is joy in the presence of the angels of God over one sinner who repents." Objects such as a small silver coin could easily be lost on the dirt and bedrock floors of Nazareth homes.

A unique feature of Nazareth is the way residents made use of its soft limestone substratum. They gouged out all types of underground repositories: spacious, multipurpose caves, cisterns for collecting rainwater, areas for storing wine, bell-shaped grain silos, and annexes to their ground-level homes. Labyrinths were often constructed by connecting these substructures with passageways and ventilation tunnels (see photo, page 69).

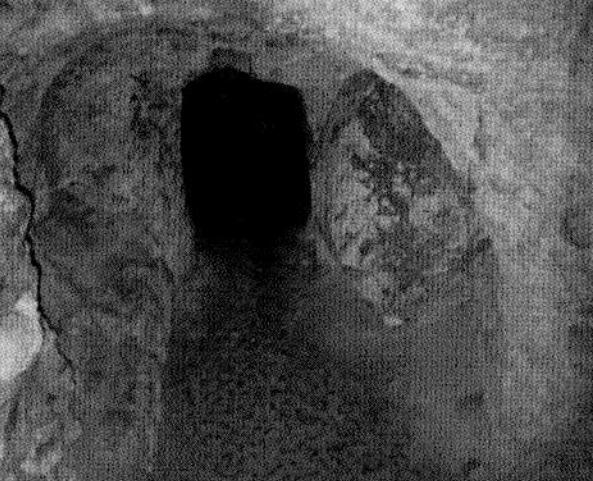

A first-century tomb discovered a short distance from the site of Mary's home. Burial plots were always outside the village; their discovery helps establish the town's boundaries.

Because Nazareth was built on a steep hillside, many homes would have had an upper and lower level and could be entered from either direction.

Multipurpose Synagogue

We know that Nazareth had a synagogue (Matthew 13:54; Mark 6:1-2; Luke 4). In Jesus' time, such synagogues served several purposes: as a courthouse, a gathering place for prayer and the reading of the Torah, a community center for conducting business and celebrations, and a school for children and youth.

In the first century, the practice of synagogues facing Jerusalem was not always observed. However, it is possible that the Nazareth synagogue did face south toward Jerusalem since the hillside town of Nazareth opens to the Valley of Jezreel in that same direction.

And Jesus increased in wisdom and in years, and in divine and human favor. —*Luke 2:52*

JESUS' HOME AND CARPENTER SHOP

Homes in a town like Nazareth did not vary much. Wealth, building location, and the trade practiced by the household were the main differences. The following pages depict the rooms and features of a home in which Jesus would have lived and worked.

Courtyard

Because the climate in Nazareth is comfortable for most of the year, much time was spent outdoors. People lived, worked, and conversed in the walled courtyard. Here they prepared, cooked, and ate meals. They tended poultry. Clothes were cleaned, woven, and mended. These activities continued till sundown signaled the time for sleep.

In some homes, a vestibule separated the courtyard from the street to help ensure privacy for the family.

Carpenter Shop

A carpenter's work area would take a good portion of the courtyard. A partial roof provided shelter from rain and sun. The carpenter's tools included hammers, chisels, planes, plumb lines, saws, axes, and adzes for shaping wood.

Carpenters built or repaired doors, furniture, plows, threshing sledges, pitchforks, yokes, and carts.

It is not known when Joseph died. His last mention in Scripture is Luke 2:51: "Then he [Jesus, age 12] went down with them [Joseph and Mary] and came to Nazareth, and was obedient to them."

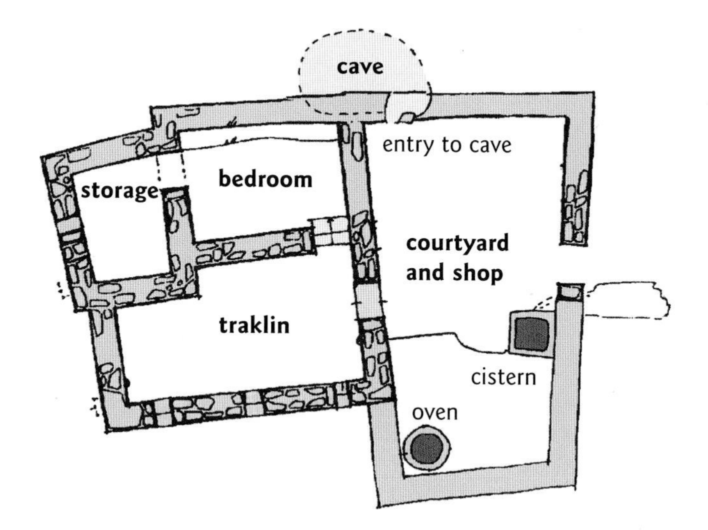

Floors were either bedrock or packed dirt. During the wet season, ash was scattered about to prevent mildew.

Common Room (Traklin)

Many homes provided a large, indoor area for family life when weather was windy, rainy, or cold. Furniture was simple and sparse.

Storage

Most homes had a small room for storing food.

Cellar

Because of the soft limestone bedrock, it was sometimes easier to add space to a home by carving a cellar than by raising walls. These hewn caves were used for additional storage and housing prized animals at night. Because they remained cool, they may also have been used to escape the midday heat.

Bedroom

A built-in loft bed could help expand the sleeping space of bedrooms, which were usually quite small and used mainly during bad weather.

Roof

The flat roof, easily accessible for a hillside home, was used for praying, drying clothes, storing flax, catching rain, and drying fruits and vegetables. During warm weather, it also offered a pleasant space to sleep.

Above: Courtyard of a home with the cistern at the lower right corner. Cisterns—sealed with plaster to prevent water loss—were usually located in the courtyard. Jewish law dictated that they be at least three handbreadths from the wall, 25 cubits from another cistern, and 50 cubits from the base of a carob or sycamore tree.

Right: Common room. Niches and small shelves were built into walls for storage and holding olive oil lamps. Windows were high, above eye level, and small enough to ensure security while still allowing light and ventilation. Windows in Nazareth homes would have used wooden shutters rather than glass panes to protect against the weather.

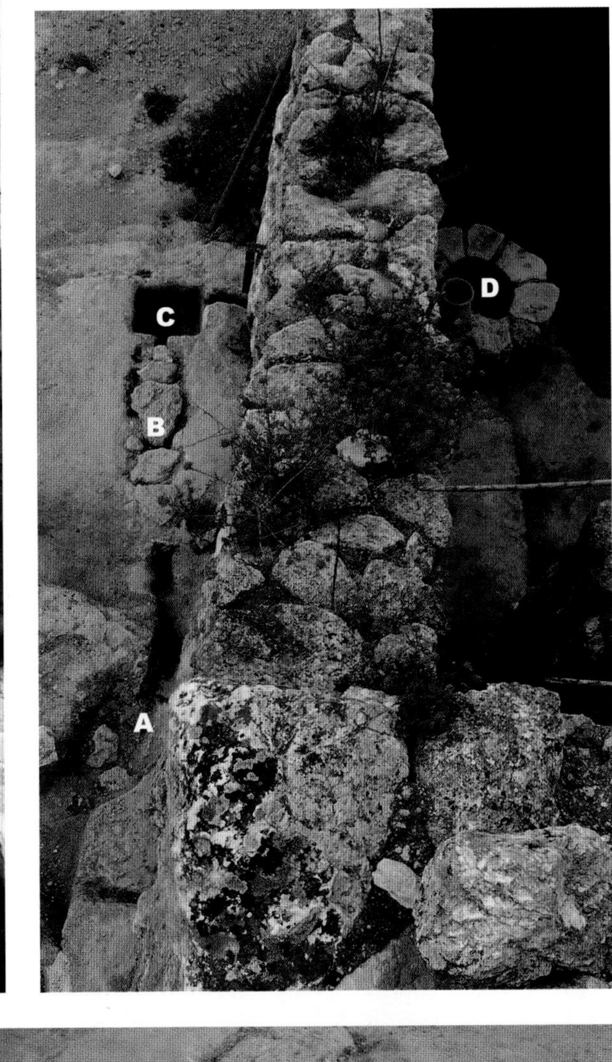

How Courtyard Water Cisterns Work

A. Water runoff from the roofs and surrounding bedrock is collected into drainage channels surrounding the house.

B. For walkways, flagstones are laid over portions of the channels.

C. Runoff flows into a sedimentation basin, letting silt settle and clear water flow to the courtyard cistern.

D. The cistern stores the water until needed for drinking, cooking, or washing. A capstone minimizes evaporation and helps keep the water clean.

Above: A view looking out from the inside of a cistern.

Left: Close-up of the sedimentation basin and the flagstones placed across the channels.

Everyone then who hears these words of mine and acts on them will be like a wise man who built his house on rock. The rain fell, the floods came, and the winds blew and beat on that house, but it did not fall, because it had been founded on rock.

—*Jesus, in Matthew 7:24-25*

BUILDING A HOUSE ON ROCK

In Matthew's Gospel, Joseph is called a carpenter (13:55). In Mark, Jesus is given that title (6:3). The Greek word is *tektōn*, which often means a carpenter or general builder.

Joseph and Jesus likely worked in stone as well as wood, building homes in their native Nazareth and in nearby Sepphoris.

Starting with a Solid Foundation

Like every first-century builder of hillside homes, they knew that one must begin by building upon the bedrock. Otherwise, winter rains will rush down the hillside in torrents, undercutting soil from beneath the foundation. With nothing to hold the walls up, one stone after another would drop out, letting the house collapse.

Nazareth Village set out to build first-century homes exactly as Joseph and Jesus would have done. While Jesus and Joseph wore different clothes and had fewer cell-phone interruptions, they built homes with these same methods and tools:

First, the foundation is cleared. Lacking power tools, first-century builders took advantage of natural dips and folds in the bedrock, converting them into walls, caves, silos, and cisterns. The site itself supplies the rock to be quarried for cornerstones and walls.

Laying the Cornerstones

Next, the cornerstones are laid, defining the dimensions of the building and anchoring the support walls. In his later ministry, Jesus offers himself as a new foundation, promising his audience that if they listen to his words and follow them, they will be building a house that will withstand the storms of life.

Raising the Walls

As the quarried stone is fit together and walls linked at the corners, rooms start to appear. While the walls of first-century homes were built quite thick (60 cm/2 ft.) for strength and insulation, the enclosed rooms were quite small, often 9 square meters or less (100 square feet). The local timber for roof beams could only span openings of about 3 meters (10 ft.).

Binding with Mortar

The building site provides the two main ingredients for mortar to fill between the stones: soil and chalk. Leftover straw from winnowing grain is mixed in to reduce cracking and increase strength. A small amount of lime can be added for improved durability.

Framing the Door

Finely quarried ashlared blocks are used for the door-jambs, thresholds, and lintels. The limestone is carved with a shahouta, or stone axe.

Adding Windows

Windows are created like miniature doorways with carved, interlocking blocks, spanned by a flat lintel stone. Many windows used in first-century Galilee were Egyptian style, narrow on the outside to keep unwanted visitors out, and opening up to the interior to allow maximum light.

Windows are concentrated on the southern and eastern walls to catch the sun as an early-morning wake-up call—and to avoid cold winter winds and driving rains, which blow in from the northwest.

Raising the Roof

Roofing begins by spanning the walls with timber beams, usually sycamore or cypress, set about 2 to 2½ meters (6½-8 ft.) above the floor. Ideally, these come from tree trunks that have survived a forest fire, which hardens the wood. The ends of the timbers could be painted with hot tar to resist decay.

Next, reeds are laid across the timbers. Sometimes these are bound together with natural fiber to hold them flat for the plaster.

A thin layer of mud plaster is then applied over the reeds. Next, a mixture of earth, ash, and chalk about 10 centimeters (4 inches) in depth is sifted over the plaster just as it begins to stiffen. It is applied dry to minimize shrinkage and cracking. The final coat is mud rich with lime to keep water from soaking through.

A heavy stone roller is used to compact and strengthen each layer. Every year the roof is weeded, checked for cracks, and re-rolled in preparation for the rainy season.

Removing the Roof

In Mark 2, four friends bring their paralyzed friend to Jesus for healing:

> And when they could not bring him to Jesus because of the crowd, they removed the roof above him; and after having dug through it, they let down the mat on which the paralytic lay. When Jesus saw their faith, he said to the paralytic, "Son, your sins are forgiven."

This could not have been done with most modern roofs. It was difficult but possible with a first-century ceiling.

The friends could not have cut through the thick ceiling beams. Fortunately, the beams were spaced about the width of a man, depending on availability of timber and the wealth of the home's owner. Though the roof was made of earth, time would have hardened it to the consistency of a well-traveled road. So unless the roof was new, the friends would have

J. Robert Teringo rendering of Sepphoris from *National Geographic*

The rebuilding of Sepphoris during Jesus' Nazareth years. To construct this city, the same carpentry and stone masonry tools and techniques were used as for a modest Nazareth home, and many of the same builders helped. This massive project took many years and required hundreds of workers from surrounding towns and villages such as Nazareth.

had to chisel through with digging irons.

Because the roof required such great effort to dig through, and even greater effort to repair, we get a sense of how committed these friends were to the paralytic, and how great their faith that Jesus could heal him.

Plastering

The last step before moving in is to plaster the interior. Small chink stones and mortar are used to fill cracks and create a flat wall surface.

The plaster is created by mixing earth and straw with chalk. Wealthier homes and public buildings, such as the Nazareth synagogue, are finished with a white lime plaster.

Plaster brightens the walls, provides insulation, prevents insects and small reptiles from invading the house, and keeps walls dry.

Give us each day our daily bread. —*Luke 11:3*

WHAT DID JESUS EAT?

In Nazareth, then as now, meals are important occasions. The act of eating and drinking together is a bond of family, friendship, and community. It is no coincidence that many of Jesus' stories and most important encounters—such as the parable of the Wedding Banquet, Feeding the Five Thousand, and the Last Supper—take place around meals or feasts.

Despite their significance, meals were quite simple and came only twice a day. Bread, legumes, oil, and dried or fresh fruit composed a typical meal.

Bread, along with water, was considered an essential of life. Except for the Sabbath, all mornings began with the women grinding wheat. Each family had a courtyard oven for baking bread. Bread was often dipped in olive oil or pureed legumes, or used as a spoon to scoop up and eat other food (as in John 13:26).

On the Sabbath, fish and vegetables would be added when available. Meat was usually limited to feast days and celebrations. A sheep fed 20 people and was slaughtered for family celebrations. A fatted calf, enough for 80, was saved for village events (see "The Prodigal Son," pages 52-55).

Among the foods most likely available in first-century Nazareth:

Grains: wheat, barley, sorghum

Legumes (pulses): lentils, broad beans, chickpeas (pulses were roasted, dried, and used in soups and stews, or ground into pastes and purees)

Vegetables: cucumbers, onions, garlic, leeks

Fruits: olives, figs, grapes, melons, pomegranates, dates (fruit by-products: olive oil, raisins, wine, dried figs, fig cakes, syrup, honey)

Nuts: walnuts, pistachios, almonds

Spices: cumin, dill, cinnamon, mint, hyssop, mallow, chicory, mustard, coriander, salt

Milk and milk by-products: butter, leben (curdled milk), yogurt, cheese

Meat and related food: eggs, fish (salted), fish by-products (fish brine, fish gravy), lamb, beef (probably quite rare), fowl (chickens, doves)

Nazareth, as a Jewish town, followed dietary laws from Hebrew Scripture governing clean and unclean animals. Cattle, sheep, and goats could be eaten. Pigs were forbidden. Fish with fins and scales were allowed. Catfish, crustaceans (crabs, lobsters, shrimp), and mollusks (clams, mussels) were not.

The last recorded meal for Jesus is in Luke 24:42-43, after his resurrection, when he eats broiled fish to show his disciples that he is not a ghost. The last meal Jesus serves is a breakfast of fish and bread (John 21).

WHAT DID JESUS WEAR?

Clothing in a small town like Nazareth was simple and functional.

The inner garment for both men and women was a tunic. Most of the year, these tunics were made from linen. In the cold and wet season, wool would be used. Tunics were often decorated with two vertical bands of color.

The outer garment was a mantle, a rectangular sheet that was wrapped about the body. Workers in the field normally took off their mantles to work. The crowds that met Jesus in Jerusalem threw their mantles to the ground for him to pass over (Mark 11:8).

In Nazareth, most clothing was likely made by weavers using traditional techniques handed down from generation to generation. Because of the large investment in raw material and labor, clothes would be patched to extend their life as long as possible.

Clothes also indicated social status. Robes were worn by the wealthy. A man's best robe symbolized his authority and was generally given to the eldest son after his death (see "The Prodigal Son," pages 52-54).

The poorest went barefoot. Those with means wore leather sandals. In wealthier homes, the sandals of guests were removed before they entered, and a servant would wash off the dust from their journey.

Men wore signet rings for sealing documents and letters. Women wore rings and necklaces.

Costumes come to life thanks to designer Grace Abdo.

A man planted a vineyard, put a fence around it, dug a pit for the wine press, and built a watchtower.
—*Mark 12:1*

THE FIELDS JESUS KNEW

In this Mark 12 parable, the vineyard Jesus describes could well be the one at Nazareth Village.

These rugged hillside terraces were tilled and tended by Nazareth farmers at the time of Jesus. The land is still called "the Vineyard" by locals, even though it has not been used as such for over a thousand years. And the first-century ruins of a winepress and watchtowers have been found.

Because this is the last remaining farmland that relates to Jesus' Nazareth, here we can best see the images that he immortalized in his parables (see pages 58-62).

Crops

Grapes and olives were the predominant crops on these terraces (see pages 36-39). Other crops grown were wheat, barley, flax, figs, and melons. Typically, vines were raised on the upper slope to avoid rotting, olive trees lower down, and grains in the valleys.

Rock Quarry to Terrace

Rock quarries generally preceded farm terraces in an area. First, rock was quarried for homes and terrace walls, leaving the hillside shaped in a stair-step pattern. Then dirt was hauled up from the valley and filled in the terraces for farming.

This process took place over many years, meaning that rock quarries were intermingled with farm terraces. In Mark 12:10 Jesus concludes his parable set in the vineyard by declaring, "The stone that the builders rejected has become the cornerstone."

A modern reader might assume that Jesus has made a sudden switch of locations. But Jesus likely was thinking of the same field—and that could well have been at Nazareth's final first-century farm, now preserved for future generations at Nazareth Village.

Nazareth, Rain, and the Quality of Mercy

The Holy Land has two seasons: rainy, from January to early April (rain can begin as early as November); and dry, when almost no rain falls.

In Matthew 5:45 Jesus says that God "sends rain on the righteous and on the unrighteous." People from rain-drenched countries often misunderstand Jesus to be saying that bad things can also happen to good people. But people in the Middle East, who realize that every drop of rain is precious, immediately understand what Jesus is saying: God's mercy is so great that even the unworthy receive it.

This rare wet-farm irrigation system discovered at Nazareth Village allowed for some crops to be watered from a spring during the dry season. Other crops survived by means of the heavy dew created when moist air blowing off the Mediterranean condensed in the cool, Nazareth nights.

The base of a watchtower, one of three found at Nazareth Village. Because farmers lived in the village, watchtowers were needed in the fields to prevent theft from people, animals, and birds during the harvest.

For first-century farmers, rocks were a nuisance to the plow. But they played an important role in dry-farm irrigation. Field rocks cooled by the sub-soil drew from the moist night air condensation that helped nurture plants during the dry season.

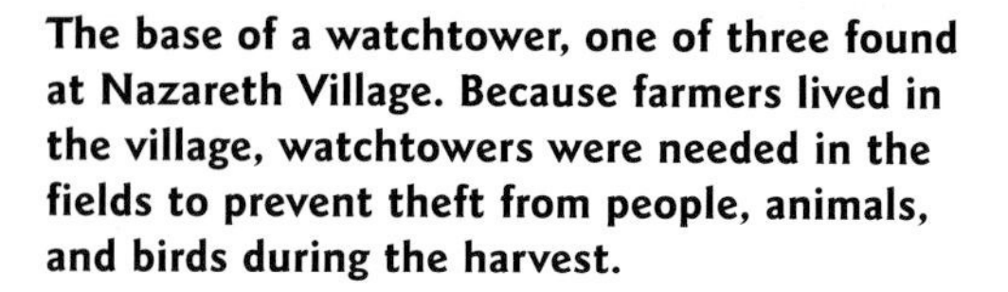

The Good Shepherd

Flocks of sheep and goats freely roamed the hills, grazing wherever grass could be found. Shepherds in Jesus' day did not drive their flocks; they led the way. The sheep, knowing and trusting their shepherd to protect them, willingly followed. First-century Galileans understood this image when Jesus compared himself to a shepherd in passages such as John 10:14: "I am the good shepherd. I know my own and my own know me."

Trees Valued for Fruit and Shade

In the Holy Land, trees are valued not only for their fruit, but also for their shade. In dry climates such as Galilee, there is a drastic difference between sun and shade. During the height of summer, the heat of the sun can quickly become unbearable. Shade and water are necessary for survival. The psalmist recognizes this in Psalm 121:5: "The Lord is your shade."

Flowers and Plants Offer Faith Lessons

In spring, the Nazareth hillsides become carpeted with a brilliant array of flowers: daisies, poppies, anemones. These flowers demonstrate both the beauty and brevity of life. Jesus turned them into a lesson of faith in Matthew 6:28-30.

Consider the lilies of the field, how they grow; they neither toil nor spin, yet I tell you, even Solomon in all his glory was not clothed like one of these. But if God so clothes the grass of the field, . . . will he not much more clothe you—you of little faith?

In describing the kingdom of God, Jesus compares it to a tiny mustard seed that grows into a plant large enough for a bird to build its nest. Jesus' audiences also knew that mustard plants would appear as a splotch of yellow on a hillside one day, and quickly spread across the entire hill, cloaking it with a brilliant yellow. In this annual act of nature, listeners could envision the spread of God's kingdom.

First-Century Farm Wages

One day's toil as a vineyard worker (a denarius) would purchase

1 seah (about 8 liters/2 gallons) of flour,
12 loaves of bread, or
1 amphora (large vase) of olive oil.

The number of days a vineyard worker would have to toil to purchase a

Ram	8 days
Calf	20 days
Ox	100 days
Lamb	4 days
Newborn donkey	3 days

Let me sing for my beloved
my love-song concerning his vineyard:
My beloved had a vineyard on a very fertile hill.
He dug it and cleared it of stones,
and planted it with choice vines;
he built a watchtower in the midst of it,
and hewed out a wine vat in it.
—*Isaiah 5:1-2*

AN AUTHENTIC FIRST-CENTURY WINEPRESS

Of all the discoveries at Nazareth Village, the most exciting is the winepress hewn into the limestone bedrock at the base of the terraces. It dramatically validates the historic name for this hillside: the Vineyard. Impressively, an archaeological evaluation has confirmed that this winepress existed at the time of Jesus.

But most of all, it is exciting because harvesting and pressing grapes was a community celebration. Imagine Jesus helping to tread grapes at this very spot! For visitors to the Holy Land who long to have their feet fall in the same imprints as Jesus', they can do no better than here.

An Exercise in Extreme Patience

Many years of work were required before a winepress could be put to use. Preparing one dunam of land (1/4 acre) for a hillside terrace took a man one year of work: clearing away stones, building walled terraces, and hauling fertile soil from the valley.

Then the vines were planted. Placing vines on

A Pressing Question
If olives can be crushed by a stone to make oil, why can't juice be extracted from grapes the same way? *Find the answer on page 39.*

The Nazareth Village winepress when first discovered. This winepress was likely used from the Roman era to Byzantine times (seventh century).

stones was the first stage toward training vines gradually onto sticks and finally upon trellises.

Each year keepers had to prune the vines, removing unfruitful branches and cutting back productive ones so that they could produce more abundantly (John 15:2, 6).

Only after three years of dressing the vines, tilling the soil, and repairing terrace walls could the first crop be harvested.

At Long Last, Harvest

Grape harvest took place in late August and September. Winepresses were created in the vineyards because it was much easier to transport the juice back to the village than heavy loads of grapes.

Winepresses were simply a large flat space carved into the bedrock. The winepress at Nazareth Village has two such spaces, separated by a narrow ridge. The presses were plastered to prevent contamination of the grapes.

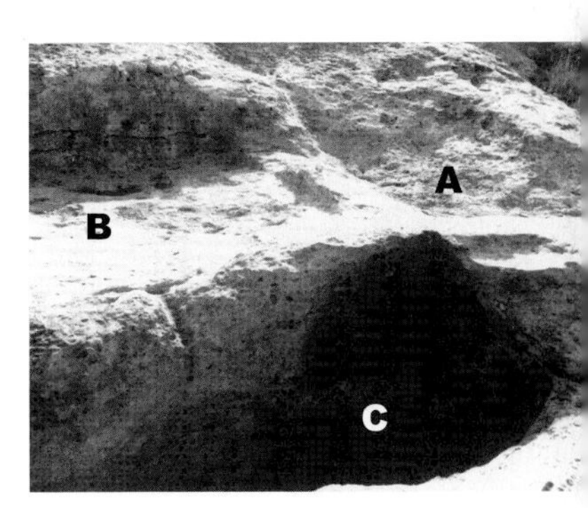

Holding onto horizontal poles suspended above their heads, grape-treaders pressed the grapes with their bare feet, separating juice from the seeds and skins. All the Nazareth villagers—men, women, and children—would help to tread out the grapes in a celebration that included hand-clapping, shouting, and singing (see Isaiah 63:2).

A channel was cut from the press to guide the juice to a lower, rock-cut pit, also plastered. From there it was dipped out and boiled into a molasses-like treacle, or processed into wine and stored in wineskins.

First-Century Nazareth Winepress (shown here before and after excavation) includes (A) holding area, (B) treading area, (C) a collection pit, and (D) water channels to collect water during the rainy season for livestock to drink.

OLIVES: MORE PRECIOUS THAN GOLD

Here at Nazareth Village, we have re-created a full-scale, first-century olive press. Each year, olives from the hundred trees on village land are harvested and pressed into oil exactly as they would have been in Jesus' day.

After being collected by hand, olives are brought to the press and placed into rings of woven palm leaves (frails) about one meter (3 ft.) across. These frails are then stacked on top of each other. A heavy crossbeam is placed over the rings. One end of the beam is anchored in the stone cliff; the other end is weighted with large stones. Then the oil is pressed out of the olives and collected in a vat, from which it is placed into jars for storage and use.

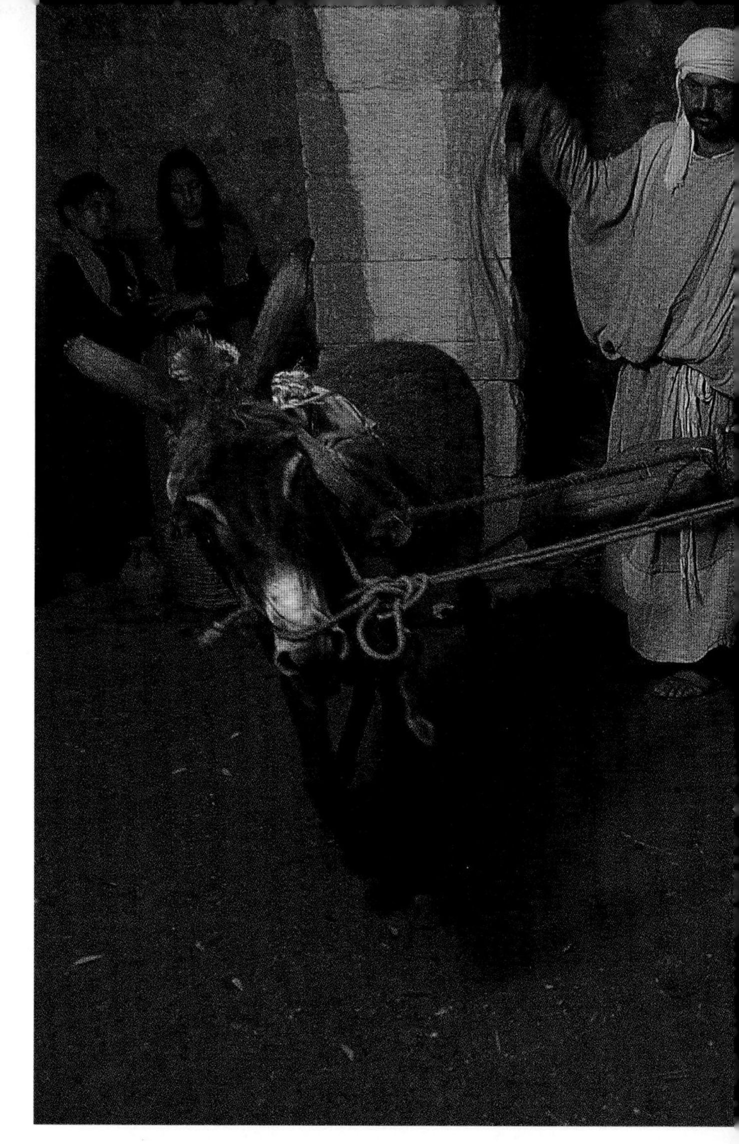

A Six-Thousand-Year Love Affair

The entire Mediterranean basin, from Spain to Syria, has had a six-millennial love affair with the olive tree and its products.

One reason is the amazing durability of olive trees. They can survive drought and floods and have been known to live more than a thousand years. Even when insects destroy the center of a tree, it survives. When cut down, it sprouts again. Whoever looks at an ancient olive tree glimpses a vision of stability, endurance, and prosperity.

Another reason is that olive oil can be used for many purposes. As an edible oil, it contains no cholesterol and is relished throughout the Middle East for cooking and as a dressing on salads.

Preserved in salt, olives can be found at any meal in the Middle East. As fuel, olive wood is hard and heavy and makes the hottest fires. Olive pits are sometimes turned into charcoal for cooking and heating.

In the carver's hands, olive wood can be made into objects of great beauty. It is little wonder that a popular local proverb says, "An abundance of olive oil brings prosperity to the house."

A Staple of Scripture

The olive tree is mentioned in the Bible more than 50 times, and its uses and meanings are many.

The olive branch in the beak of a dove was the

Answer to a Pressing Question
A crushing stone does not affect the flavor of olive oil. Because the grape seed is bitter, however, crushing with a hard, heavy stone would ruin the wine. Soft-padded feet, then, are the perfect instruments for extracting juice from a grape without smashing the seed.

sign to Noah that the flood was over and that life would go on. From this story the olive branch has become a symbol of peace and reconciliation.

Hosea prophesies that the people of God will be beautiful like the olive (14:6). Jeremiah (11:16) tells his listeners:

The Lord once called you, "A green olive tree, fair with goodly fruit."

Used in medicine, olive oil was an antidote for poison and an agent for cleaning wounds, as recounted in the parable of the Good Samaritan. (Luke 10:30-37).

Olive oil was used by the wealthy to clean themselves and for anointing the head. This practice is referred to in the story of the woman in the house of Simon (Luke 7:46; also, Psalm 23:5).

As a base for fragrant ointments, olive oil was used to anoint kings (1 Samuel 10:1) and indeed was used to anoint Jesus at the beginning of Holy Week. The women who gathered on Easter morning wanted to anoint Jesus' body with a similar oil-based perfume, but could not do so, because the body was not in the tomb. So olive oil played a part in the beginning and the end of the great events of Holy Week.

A Light That Conquers Night

Olive oil has been used in clay lamps to provide light in homes for at least six millennia.

Jesus urges his disciples to boldly proclaim the good news:

You are the light of the world. . . . No one after lighting a lamp puts it under the bushel basket, but on the lampstand, and it gives light to all in the house. —*Matthew 5:14-15*

A flame fueled by olive oil is the image Jesus has in mind when he announces himself as a light in the darkness:

I have come as light into the world, so that everyone who believes in me should not remain in the darkness. —*John 12:46*

NAZARETH VILLAGE

A first-century farm and village presenting the life, times, and teachings of Jesus of Nazareth for all the world.

For everything there is a season,
and a time for every matter under heaven:
a time to be born, and a time to die;
a time to plant, and a time to pluck up
what is planted. —*Ecclesiastes 3:1-2*

A DAY AND YEAR IN THE LIFE OF FIRST-CENTURY NAZARETH

DAY	EVENTS
Before dawn	Grinding grain and baking bread begins.
First light	Work begins in fields and courtyards (when working in Sepphoris, Joseph and Jesus begin their hour commute by foot).
Early morning	Women draw water from well, exchange news.
Late morning	First meal.
Midday	Rest in the heat of day (noon till three), after which work resumes.
Late afternoon	Women again draw water from well.
Workday ends	Hour journey back from Sepphoris for Joseph and Jesus.
Evening	Second meal (usually long and leisurely, a time of conversation and fellowship).
Sunset	Soon to sleep. Nighttime activity is kept at a minimum to conserve lamp fuel.
Night	During harvest, the night is divided into three watches, with villagers taking shifts in the watchtowers to safeguard crops.

Sabbath is from sundown on Friday to sundown on Saturday. During these hours the villagers suspend ordinary work and spend time in fellowship and worship.

Daylight is divided into twelve equal parts; hence, an "hour" in the summer is longer than an "hour" in winter. The first hour is reckoned by the beginning of sunrise, the sixth hour around noon, the eleventh hour marks the final hour of light.

YEAR	EVENTS
September	Harvest of olives begins. Rosh Hashanah, New Year (Sept./Oct.).
October	Feast of Tabernacles. Plowing begins.
November	Sowing of wheat, barley begins.
December	Sowing of peas, lentils, flax. Feast of Lights (Hanukkah).
January	Heaviest rains begin, assisting the growing of winter crops.
February	Feast of Purim, Adar 14-15 (Feb./Mar.).
March	Flax harvest begins.
April	Dry season begins. Passover, travel to Jerusalem. Harvest of barley, peas, lentils begins.
May	Vine tending and wheat harvest begins.
June	Wheat harvest ends. Pentecost.
July	Hoeing of fields.
August	Harvest of summer fruits begins (grapes, figs, pomegranates).

The Jewish lunar calendar has twelve months, though they do not align with those of the solar calendar. For instance, Kislev spans parts of November and December, and includes Hanukkah. Because the short Jewish year has only about 354 days, the addition of a thirteenth month (Adar Sheni/WeAdar, "second Adar") is required every three to four years.

TO NAZARETH, FROM A WORLD OF DARKNESS

It is easy to think of first-century Nazareth and Galilee as a quiet refuge, isolated from the tragedy and conflict of Jerusalem and the nation at large. But that was not the case, nor had it been for centuries.

On his way to conquer Egypt, Alexander the Great marched along the Mediterranean coast. Invading armies lived off the land and pillaged small farming villages like Nazareth.

After Alexander's death in 323 BC, Galilee became a football, fought over by Greek rulers from Alexandria, Egypt, to the south, and Antioch, Syria, to the north.

In 175 BC, one of Antioch's rulers, Antiochus IV, took control and the title of Epiphanes, "[God] Manifest." Antiochus then decided that all the people in his kingdom should accept Greek civilization.

Religious Oppression and Revolt

In Jewish provinces, the Syrian Greeks burned all copies of the law they found, stopped sacrificial offerings, and forbade all Jewish religious practices. The Jews resisted, and conflict broke out. In 167 BC, the Greeks took over the temple in Jerusalem, dedicated it to the pagan god Zeus, and sacrificed pigs on its altar.

After a time of bloody persecution, a resistance movement rose out of Judea. The fighters were called the Maccabeans. Fighting a successful guerrilla war, they managed to win partial (164 BC) and eventually full (142) independence.

But soon the resistors began fighting among themselves, and the land was ravaged again and again. As a result, when the Romans arrived a half-century before the time of Jesus, they conquered the land with ease (63 BC).

Yet great civil unrest continued. The Romans appointed the son of the family called Herod to be king of the Jews (40 BC), but it took him three years to conquer the kingdom before he could rule it.

MARY, BLESSED AMONG WOMEN

All that Scripture tells us about Mary, the mother of Jesus, is that she lived in Nazareth and was engaged to a builder named Joseph, a descendant of King David. Mary was perhaps14-16 years old and a virgin when the angel Gabriel appeared to announce that she would bear a son to be named Jesus. Facing possible abandonment by Joseph and public disgrace, how did Mary respond? With amazing faith: "Here am I, the servant of the Lord; let it be with me according to your word" (Luke 1:38). When Elizabeth (then pregnant with John the Baptist) heard Mary's greeting, the child leaped in Elizabeth's womb, and Mary's relative exclaimed with a loud cry, "Blessed are you among women, and blessed is the fruit of your womb" (Luke 1:42).

Herod Rules with an Iron Fist

Conquer and rule it he did, with a brutal, iron fist. On a daily basis Herod the Great executed those who threatened his rule, often hundreds at a time. So his slaughter of all the male babies in Bethlehem—a massacre the infant Jesus escaped—would have made little impression on the general population (Matthew 2). Before he was finished, Herod had murdered his brother-in-law, his favorite wife, and three of his sons.

All during this period there was, at one time or another, conflict with the Armenians and Parthians to the north and northeast, and with the Nabateans to the south.

As a province, Galilee also produced resistance fighters, and Herod fought ruthlessly to defeat them. He lowered armed soldiers protected by iron chests down to the entrances of cliff caves and slaughtered the rebels in their hideouts.

After Herod's death (4 BC), a revolt against Rome broke out in Galilee. Varus, the Roman governor in Damascus, descended on the province, ordering the crucifixion of thousands. In this conflict Sepphoris, the city just north of Nazareth, was completely destroyed.

Could any new voice for compassion and justice be raised in a country exhausted and traumatized by three centuries of mindless brutality?

During the time of Jesus, thousands of dissidents preceded him to Roman crosses.

Nazareth and New Responses

The town of Nazareth was born during this turbulent time. Many scholars have suggested that the community was founded, perhaps around 100 BC, by Jews sent from Judea to reclaim and rebuild Galilee as a Jewish province after centuries of occupation.

When the young child Jesus arrived with Joseph and Mary, Nazareth was probably inhabited by descendants of those original immigrants from Judea.

At the time Jesus was growing up in Nazareth, the people of this beleaguered land responded in different ways to the brutality of daily life. Some became political and military activists and opposed Roman rule with violence.

Others chose to live quiet lives, studying the Torah. They formed clubs in the villages and called themselves Khaberim (companions). The Pharisees related to this movement.

Still others decided to retreat into the desert. There they could preserve their culture and traditions and wait for a purified temple and priesthood. They were from the Essenes.

A group of aristocratic priests concentrated on the temple and its rituals and fiercely opposed any new theological developments. They were known as the Sadducees.

The ruling empire of Rome brought roads, aqueducts—and death to any who dared to stand in their way.

As mighty as their empire was, Rome was wary of this remote corner of the world. And rebellion is what Rome feared most. Its powerful Tenth Legion kept a watchful eye on the place where previous revolutions had their roots: Galilee.

The world was sorely in need of hope—a light to overcome the darkness (Matthew 4:15–16; John 1:4-5).

THE ANNUNCIATION

(from Luke 1)

The Birth of Jesus Foretold

In the sixth month the angel Gabriel was sent by God to a town in Galilee called Nazareth, to a virgin engaged to a man whose name was Joseph, of the house of David. The virgin's name was Mary.

And he came to her and said, "Greetings, favored one! The Lord is with you." But she was much perplexed by his words and pondered what sort of greeting this might be.

The angel said to her, "Do not be afraid, Mary, for you have found favor with God. And now, you will conceive in your womb and bear a son, and you will name him Jesus. He will be great, and will be called the Son of the Most High, and the Lord God will give to him the throne of his ancestor David. He will reign over the house of Jacob forever, and of his kingdom there will be no end."

Mary said to the angel, "How can this be, since I am a virgin?"

The angel said to her, "The Holy Spirit will come upon you, and the power of the Most High will overshadow you; therefore the child to be born will be holy; he will be called Son of God."

Then Mary said, "Here am I, the servant of the Lord; let it be with me according to your word." Then the angel departed from her.

Mary's Song of Praise

And Mary said,

"My soul magnifies the Lord,
and my spirit rejoices in God my Savior,
for he has looked with favor on
the lowliness of his servant.

"Surely, from now on all generations
will call me blessed;
for the Mighty One has done great things for me,
and holy is his name.

"His mercy is for those who fear him
from generation to generation.

"He has shown strength with his arm;
he has scattered the proud in the
thoughts of their hearts.

"He has brought down the powerful
from their thrones,
and lifted up the lowly;
he has filled the hungry with good things,
and sent the rich away empty.

"He has helped his servant Israel,
in remembrance of his mercy,
according to the promise he made
to our ancestors,
to Abraham and to his
descendants forever."

Various traditions hold that the angel Gabriel appeared to Mary at her home, which today lies under the Basilica of the Annunciation (far left and above left), or at Mary's Well, in the Church of Saint Gabriel (above), at the opposite end of the original town.

Today this scripture has been fulfilled in your hearing. —*Jesus, in Luke 4:21*

THE INAUGURATION

When Jesus was twelve, a choice had to be made whether or not he should become a scholar, spending all his spare time at the Nazareth synagogue studying and discussing Scripture.

We know from Jesus' sophisticated knowledge of Scripture that he did become a scholar. And we know that, in time, Jesus was referred to as Rabbi, or Teacher. One did not get this title from attending a special school, but out of respect from one's community.

Because Jesus worked as a carpenter and told stories, we sometimes assume he was a simple peasant. But in the East, scholars use stories to debate truth and law, much like conceptual thought is used in the West.

Jesus would have been expected to continue his trade so that Scripture did not become a spade to dig with for money. Also, because the law dealt with everyday life, a teacher of the law was expected to be familiar with problems faced by others.

Jesus was possibly part of the religious study fellowship called Khaberim (the companions), a group associated with the Pharisees. These associates studied the Scriptures and sought to apply them to their troubled times.

Jesus Returns to Nazareth

In his early 30s, Jesus sets out from Nazareth to begin his ministry. Luke 4 records that, after a short time, Jesus returns to Nazareth, goes to the synagogue on the Sabbath, as was his custom, and is given the scroll of the prophet Isaiah to read.

This is a big moment for Nazareth. Here is their hometown hero. They have heard great things about his teaching and healing throughout Galilee. What passage will Jesus read? How will he interpret it?

When the Torah is read in the synagogue, rabbis are required to read word for word. But when reading from the prophets, such as Isaiah, some freedom is allowed. The reader can drop a line, add a word, or borrow a phrase from another part of Scripture, providing it doesn't require too much turning of the scroll.

As Jesus reads, he does all these to shape four points: (1) the proclamation of the good news, (2) a cry for justice, (3) a call for compassion, and (4) announcing that he is the anointed one of God.

What Jesus Reads

Jesus starts with Isaiah 61:1-2: "The Spirit of the Lord is upon me, because he has anointed me."

To be anointed in this case means to be the Messiah. Thus, Jesus affirms that the Spirit of the Lord is upon him and that he is the Messiah of God.

He then reads: "To bring good news to the poor." Here Jesus is proclaiming good news to the humble who seek God (Isaiah 66:2) and calling for an economic transformation of society, a Jubilee to relieve the heavy burden of the impoverished.

The next phrase announces: "He has sent me to proclaim release to the captives." Then, with a turn of the scroll to 58:6, Jesus adds, "To let the oppressed go free." This is talking about justice for the captives and the oppressed.

Finally, in the center of the Luke text we have an act of healing and compassion: "And recovery of sight to the blind."

So Jesus has established that he is the Spirit-filled Messiah of God, and that his ministry is proclamation of the gospel, justice advocacy, and compassion.

Luke then writes that Jesus "rolled up the scroll, gave it back to the attendant, and sat down."

Jesus was sitting on "Moses' seat," reserved for the teacher. So everyone was looking at him, waiting for him to interpret the Scripture reading.

What Jesus Does Not Read

Because Nazareth was founded as part of an effort to reclaim Galilee from the Gentiles, many in the audience are likely disappointed at what Jesus fails to read from Isaiah 61: "They shall build up the

The cliff from which the villagers tried to toss Jesus could have been small, like the one we see here before the synagogue. The Mishnah (Sanhedrin 6:4) specifies that those found guilty of a capital offense are to be taken to the brink of a cliff twice the height of a man. The blasphemer is then to be thrown down headfirst. If the fall fails to kill him, the witnesses are to finish the job by casting down stones on him.

ancient ruins. . . . Strangers shall . . . feed your flocks, foreigners shall till your land and dress your vines." In other words, the people who now rule over you will be your servants.

Still, Jesus' audience remains supportive. "All spoke well of him and were amazed at the gracious words that came out of his mouth."

But the people in Jesus' audience want to know what benefits he will bring them. This popular teacher, after all, is one of their own.

Jesus answers by telling two stories from the Hebrew Scriptures. One is a story of the widow at Zarephath near Sidon, in the days of Elijah. The other is the account of Naaman the Syrian, who was healed of his leprosy by Elisha. Both were Gentiles, and each made a costly decision of faith to obey God speaking through a prophet.

A Foreshadowing of the Cross

The audience is stunned. Jesus—their Jesus!—is not only refusing to reassure them that their enemies will be driven out of Galilee or enslaved; he is also asking them to learn the meaning of faith from these despised Gentiles, to accept that God's favor is no longer theirs alone but is now to be extended to all the world—even to enemies!

This is too much. This goes beyond insolence. It is heresy. The audience becomes enraged and decides to kill Jesus. "They . . . led him to the brow of the hill on which their town was built, so that they might hurl him off the cliff." But by the power of Jesus' presence, he passes through the mob and walks away.

In this passage, we can glimpse the foreshadowing of both the cross and the resurrection.

Beyond the Annunciation, this Inauguration—Jesus' appearance at the Nazareth synagogue in Luke 4—is the only major scene from all the Gospels that we know took place in Nazareth. It is also one of the most important Gospel scenes: Jesus announcing God's program for his messianic ministry.

Here in his own hometown Jesus thrills, shocks, and scandalizes by revealing that he is anointed by God, not to bring worldly political power to a chosen few, but to share God's good news with all, including the poor, the oppressed, and outsiders, considered at that time to be impure and unworthy of God's blessing.

THE PRODIGAL SON
Through First-Century Ears

(Luke 15:11-32 as told by Dr. Nakhle Bishara)

Then Jesus said: A man had two sons. The younger demanded, "Father, give me my inheritance." So the father divided his property between them.

The audience listening to Jesus will think, "How could a son be so rude as to ask for his inheritance while his father is still alive?" To ask for your inheritance is to wish your father dead! This is a big insult. But then the story becomes even more impossible.

The younger brother then gathered all that he had and traveled to a distant country.

Life at that time was always within a community. Always! Leaving community to live with foreigners means going into exile. Such an alien, a wanderer, doesn't have the same respect, or rights. Here the story and the Prodigal Son's rebellion against his father's authority touches on Adam and Eve. Their original sin was to separate from God because they thought they could do better on their own.

The pods fed to the pigs were likely carob pods. Only the poorest would have considered eating them.

When he had squandered everything, a famine struck. So the younger brother hired himself out to feed pigs.

Now he has degraded himself even more by caring for filthy animals considered ritually unclean. The younger son has now done three of the worst things this audience can imagine, so they will be listening closely to what Jesus says next.

He would have been happy for the pods the pigs were eating, but he was given nothing. So he said to himself, "How many of my father's slaves have bread to spare while I am dying of hunger? I will return to my father and say, 'Father, I have sinned against heaven and before you. I am no longer worthy to be called your son. Treat me like one of your slaves.'"

Maybe the exiled son had a true repentance, but he is also making a calculation: If I go back, even if I am treated as a slave, I will be better off. So this parable retells the story of the Hebrew Scriptures—the fall of humanity, life in exile, and finally the desire to return home and be delivered from our miserable condition.

So the younger brother headed back to his father. But while he was still far off, his father saw him and was filled with compassion.

Because the father saw his son while he was far away, the father was probably sitting on his flat roof and watching the road that led to the village, hoping that his lost son would come back someday. Here is the story of God's initiative to reconcile us.

The father ran and put his arms around his son and kissed him on the neck.

On the cross, Jesus was humiliated so that the human race could be reconciled. Here we see that same humiliation on the part of the father. In Eastern culture, to rush is not dignified. A dignified person would walk slowly. And then the father falls on his son's neck. It should have been the other way around. Equal people kiss on the cheek. If someone is of lower status, he falls on the neck or the shoulder of his superior. If he is of even lower status, he

should kiss the hand. And if he is a slave, he would kiss the feet.

Then the son said, "Father, I have sinned against heaven and before you. I am no longer worthy to be called your son." But the father said to his servants, "Quickly, bring out my best robe and put it on him."

The father does not let his son end the speech as he planned, with "Treat me like one of your slaves." Instead, he calls for his best robe, a sign of highest honor. When a dignified person dies, the family will come and take that robe and put it over the eldest son as a sign that now all the respect belongs to him.

"Put a ring on his finger and sandals on his feet."

The ring adds to this: a signet ring means the son is able to sign in the father's name. Even after the terrible things the younger son has done! And only slaves would go barefoot! So by giving him sandals, the father is saying, "My son is a free man, with all his rights exactly as before." The signet ring is also used as a symbol of authority in the story of Joseph and the Pharaoh (Genesis 41:41-42). But the story is not yet finished.

"And get the fatted calf and kill it. Let us eat and celebrate, for this son of mine was dead and is alive again. He was lost and is found."

The father has reconciled with his son, but that is not enough. Now the father takes initiative to reconcile his son with the village—his community. We know this because for the feast he slaughters a calf, not a sheep. A sheep would feed only about 20 people. A calf would feed 80. But our story still is not complete.

Now the eldest son became angry when he learned what had happened. And he said to his father, "For all these years I have never disobeyed your command, yet you have not given me even a goat so I could celebrate with my friends." Then the father said to him, "Son, all that I have is yours. But we must rejoice because your brother was dead and has come to life. He was lost and has been found."

Dr. Nakhle Bishara told this story from Luke 15 to illustrate the need for a place where visitors could hear the stories of Jesus in the same way they were heard and understood by those who lived in Jesus' day.

To contrast human justice with heavenly justice, Jesus ends with the eldest son. Human justice is "an eye for an eye" as the eldest brother understood things. Instead of receiving back all his rights, his younger brother should be punished. But heavenly justice is full of compassion and utmost mercy. It is life instead of death. It is being found rather than remaining lost.

In this one amazing story, we are assured that God watches out for the lost and welcomes them back with open arms.

If all of Scripture would disappear so that only the story of the Prodigal Son remains, we would still have all the story of our relationship with God from the beginning.

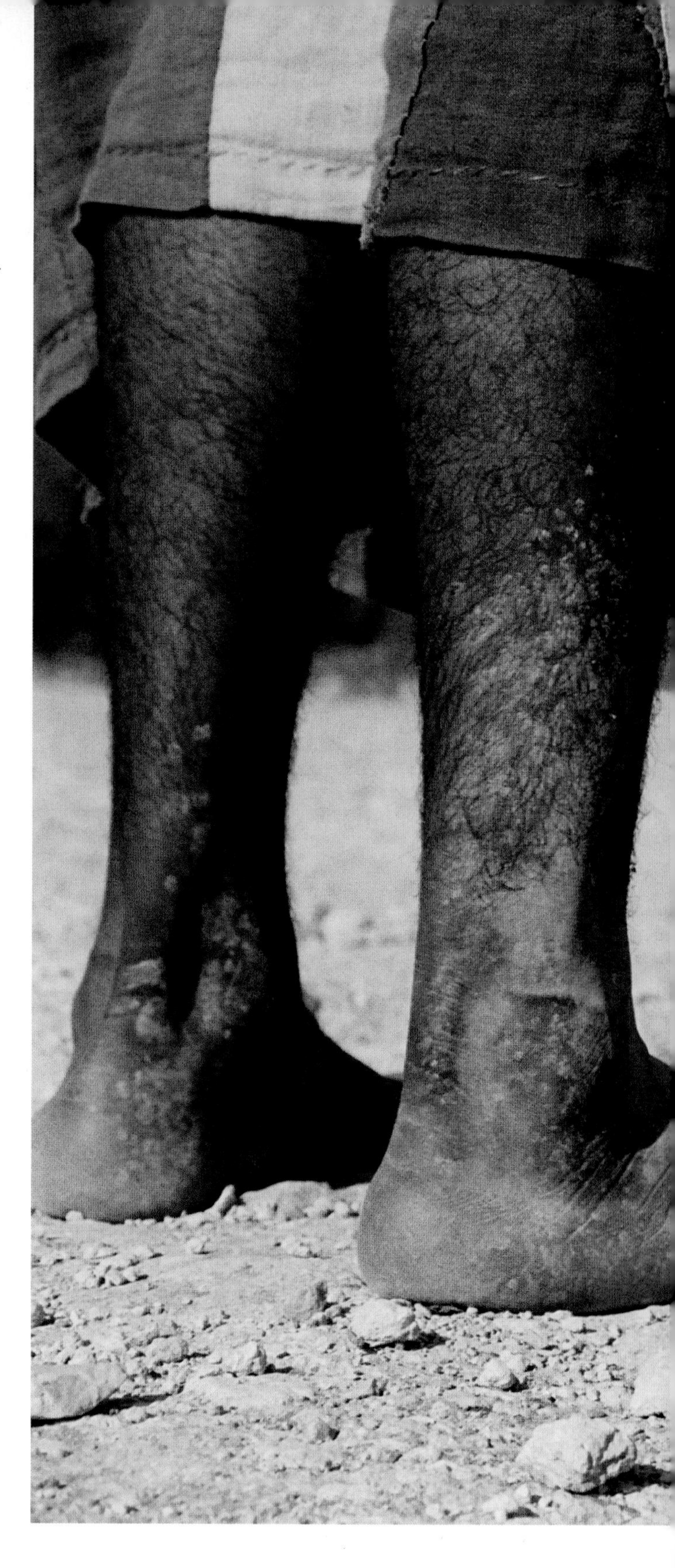

NAZARETH IN THE GOSPELS

Annunciation

In the sixth month the angel Gabriel was sent by God to a town in Galilee called Nazareth, to a virgin engaged to a man whose name was Joseph, of the house of David. The virgin's name was Mary. —*Luke 1:26-27*

And Mary remained with [Elizabeth] about three months and then returned to her home. —*Luke 1:56*

Birth and Childhood

Joseph also went from the town of Nazareth in Galilee to Judea, to the city of David called Bethlehem, because he was descended from the house and family of David. —*Luke 2:4*

Then Joseph got up, took the child and his mother, and went to the land of Israel. But when he heard that Archelaus was ruling over Judea in place of his father Herod, he was afraid to go there. And after being warned in a dream, he went away to the district of Galilee. There he made his home in a town called Nazareth, so that what had been spoken through the prophets might be fulfilled, "He will be called a Nazorean." —*Matthew 2:21-23*

When [Joseph, Mary, and the child Jesus] had finished everything required by the law of the Lord, they returned to Galilee, to their own town of Nazareth. The child grew and became strong, filled with wisdom; and the favor of God was upon him. —*Luke 2:39*

[Jesus] said to [Joseph and Mary], "Why were you searching for me? Did you not know that I must be in my Father's house?" But they did not understand what he said to them. Then he went down with them and came to Nazareth, and was obedient to them. His mother treasured all these things in her heart. —*Luke 2:49-51*

Inauguration

In those days Jesus came from Nazareth of Galilee and was baptized by John in the Jordan. —*Mark 1:9*

[Jesus] left that place and came to his hometown, and his disciples followed him. —*Mark 6:1*

[Jesus] came to his hometown and began to teach the people in their synagogue, so that they were astounded and said, "Where did this man get this wisdom and these deeds of power?" —*Matthew 13:54*

When [Jesus] came to Nazareth, where he had been brought up, he went to the synagogue on the Sabbath day, as was his custom. —*Luke 4:16*

[Jesus] said to them, "Doubtless you will quote to me this proverb, 'Doctor, cure yourself!' And you will say, 'Do here also in your hometown the things that we have heard you did at Capernaum.'" And he said, "Truly I tell you, no prophet is accepted in the prophet's hometown." —*Luke 4:23-24*

They got up, drove [Jesus] out of the town, and led him to the brow of the hill on which their town was built, so that they might hurl him off the cliff. —*Luke 4:29*

Ministry

Philip found Nathanael and said to him, "We have found him about whom Moses in the law and also the prophets wrote, Jesus son of Joseph from Nazareth." Nathanael said to him, "Can anything good come out of Nazareth?" Philip said to him, "Come and see." —*John 1:45-46*

Now when Jesus heard that John had been arrested, he withdrew to Galilee. He left Nazareth and made his home in Capernaum by the sea, in the territory of Zebulun and Naphtali. —*Matthew 4:12-13*

Just then there was in their synagogue a man with an unclean spirit, and he cried out, "What have you to do with us, Jesus of Nazareth? Have you come to destroy us? I know who you are, the Holy One of God." —*Mark 1:23-24; Luke 4:33-34*

Bartimaeus son of Timaeus, a blind beggar, was sitting by the roadside. When he heard that it was Jesus of Nazareth, he began to shout out and say, "Jesus, Son of David, have mercy on me!" —*Mark 10:46-47; Luke 18:35-38*

Death and Resurrection

When he entered Jerusalem, the whole city was in turmoil, asking, "Who is this?" The crowds were saying, "This is the prophet Jesus from Nazareth in Galilee." —*Matthew 21:10-11*

Then Jesus, knowing all that was to happen to him, came forward and asked them, "Whom are you looking for?" They answered, "Jesus of Nazareth." Jesus replied, "I am he." Judas, who betrayed him, was standing with them. When Jesus said to them, "I am he," they stepped back and fell to the ground. Again he asked them, "Whom are you looking for?" And they said, "Jesus of Nazareth." —*John 18:4-7*

Now Peter was sitting outside in the courtyard. A servant-girl came to him and said, "You also were with Jesus the Galilean." But he denied it before all of them, saying, "I do not know what you are talking about." When he went out to the porch, another servant-girl saw him, and she said to the bystanders, "This man was with Jesus of Nazareth." —*Matthew 26:69-71; Mark 14:66-67*

There they crucified him, and with him two others, one on either side, with Jesus between them. Pilate also had an inscription written and put on the cross. It read, "Jesus of Nazareth, the King of the Jews." —*John 19:18-19*

As [Mary Magdalene, and Mary the mother of James, and Salome] entered the tomb, they saw a young man, dressed in a white robe, sitting on the right side; and they were alarmed. But he said to them, "Do not be alarmed; you are looking for Jesus of Nazareth, who was crucified. He has been raised; he is not here. Look, there is the place they laid him." —*Mark 16:5-6*

[Jesus] asked them, "What things?" They replied, "The things about Jesus of Nazareth, who was a prophet mighty in deed and word before God and all the people." —*Luke 24:19*

Art by Elizabeth Swindle

NAZARETH THROUGH THE MIRROR OF THE PARABLES

Nazareth can be seen through all the Gospels, reflected as if by a mirror in the images Jesus uses and the stories he tells. Nowhere is this more evident than in his parables.

And nowhere are the parables more evident than on the hillside terraces at Nazareth Village.

Olive Tree Parable

The trees once went out to anoint a king over themselves. So they said to the olive tree, "Reign over us." The olive tree answered them, "Shall I stop producing my rich oil by which gods and mortals are honored, and go to sway over the trees?"—*Judges 9:8-9*

Following the way of the Hebrew prophets such as Jeremiah, Ezekiel, and Isaiah, Jesus used creative stories filled with dramatic action to convey spiritual truth in a manner that his audience could understand and accept.

Vineyard Parables

Then [Jesus] began to speak to them in parables. "A man planted a vineyard, put a fence around it, dug a pit for the winepress, and built a watchtower; then he leased it to tenants and went to another country.

"When the season came, he sent a slave to the tenants to collect from them his share of the produce of the vineyard. But they seized him, and beat him, and sent him away empty-handed.

"And again he sent another slave to them; this one they beat over the head and insulted. Then he sent another, and that one they killed. And so it was with many others; some they beat, and others they killed.

"He had still one other, a beloved son. Finally he sent him to them, saying, 'They will respect my son.'"
—*Mark 12:1-6*

When Jesus created this story, he was actually retelling a parable told by Isaiah the prophet. In Isaiah 5, the parable is called a love-song. The singer is the prophet and the lover is God. The lover starts a vineyard on a hill much like the one at Nazareth Village. He builds the terraces and plants them with choice vines. But alas! The vineyard produces worthless wild grapes.

The parable then becomes a story of judgment as the prophet says, with some powerful wordplay (5:7):

> God expected justice [mish-pat],
> but saw bloodshed [mish-pakh];
> righteousness [tse-da-qah],
> but heard a cry! [tse-'a-qah].

God wanted justice but found bloodshed. God wanted righteousness but was faced with a cry from the oppressed.

Now near the end of his ministry, Jesus retells Isaiah's parable, but with critical differences. By introducing a new character, the son of the vineyard owner, Jesus places himself at the center of the story.

Jesus tells how the owner rents his vineyard to tenants, who refuse to pay. He sends a series of servants to the renters, but they are badly mistreated. So the owner decides to send his "beloved son."

The son makes his way to the renters, coming alone and unarmed, with total vulnerability, hoping to obtain the renters' obedience. Will the renters'

response to the unarmed appearance of the owner's son be justice (mish-pat) and righteousness (tse-da-qah)? Or will it be bloodshed (mish-pakh) and a cry (tse-'a-qah)?

"But those tenants said to one another, 'This is the heir; come, let us kill him, and the inheritance will be ours.'

"So they seized him, killed him, and threw him out of the vineyard. What then will the owner of the vineyard do? He will come and destroy the tenants and give the vineyard to others." —*Mark 12:7-9*

Across the centuries, Christian interpreters have seen in this vineyard parable a window into the mystery of the cross.

The Parable of the Sower

A sower went out to sow. And as he sowed, some seeds fell on the path, and the birds came and ate them up. Other seeds fell on rocky ground, where they did not have much soil, and they sprang up quickly, since they had no depth of soil. But when the sun rose, they were scorched; and since they had no root, they with-

ered away. Other seeds fell among thorns, and the thorns grew up and choked them. Other seeds fell on good soil and brought forth grain, some a hundredfold, some sixty, some thirty. Let anyone with ears listen!
—*Matthew 13:3-9*

Those familiar with modern farms may think that this sower is careless. But when visitors to Nazareth walk these narrow terraces and feel the strong winds that rush up from the valleys, they understand that it is not possible for any farmer to cast every precious seed on fertile soil.

Despite his best efforts, some seed falls along the hard path that farmers use to reach their fields. Because the seed cannot be plowed under, birds eat it. Other seed falls on "rocky ground." This does not mean ground full of fieldstones that a lazy farmer has not bothered to clear away. Rather, it refers to ground where the underlying rock is close to the surface. The soil is too shallow. When it rains, this soil remains wet and the seeds germinate more quickly. The sun follows closely after the rain, drying the soil, and the plants, because they can establish no deep roots, soon die.

Some seed falls among thorns, and the thorns choke the plants that sprout. As any farmer knows, weeds that spread by extending their roots underground are almost impossible to kill, even by chopping them out. So first-century farmers without herbicides could only endure these highly aggressive thistles and thorns.

And some seeds fall on good ground and bring forth abundant fruit—astoundingly, even up to a hundredfold.

Because the audience knows first-century farming, they understand what Jesus is saying in this deceptively simple parable:

1. Jesus is encouraging his listeners to receive the good seed of God's good news with fertile spirits.

2. The kingdom of God does not come with a political revolution, as many expected. Nor does it begin with the stars falling from the sky and the sun refusing to shine, as the visionaries predicted. Instead, the kingdom of God comes like a seed growing slowly and quietly in soft, deep, clean soil.

Parable of the Great Banquet

In another parable (Luke 14:15-24), Jesus talks about the great banquet that the Messiah is expected to spread for all believers at the end of history.

In this parable, a man plans a banquet and invites many. On the day of the banquet, the host prepares everything and sends his servant out to summon the guests.

Those who are summoned begin to make excuses.

The Gospel of Luke presents the excuses in vivid detail. One of them relates to the field we see pictured in the photo below. The guest says, "I have bought a piece of land, and I must go out and see it; please accept my regrets."

Knowing land, Jesus' audience immediately understands that this excuse is intended as a humiliating, public insult. No one in this time and place would ever buy land that he has not seen.

Is it worthless bedrock, like the plot pictured below at the bottom of the photo? Or is it a finished field, as in the center, constructed and maintained by a generation of backbreaking work, with terraces and retaining walls in good shape, ready for planting?

The host has the right to become angry at the invited guests. His natural response would be to seek revenge. But he does neither. Instead, he turns his anger into grace by inviting the "poor and the lame" to take their place.

With this parable, Jesus is claiming that meals with him are the beginning of the messianic banquet promised in Isaiah 25:6-8. Some leaders in the community refuse to attend Jesus' banquet. They imagine that the banquet will fail when they don't appear. Jesus' response, like the host in the parable, is to reprocess his anger into grace as he calls the outcasts of the community to the banquet instead.

Throughout history, great injustice has been inflicted on many people across our world. Injustice creates great energy. What is to be done with the energy created by injustice? In this parable, Jesus gives his answer.

Living Water at the Well

Anyone who has lived in the Middle East knows that water is a rare and precious commodity. Every day, it determines life or death. In Jesus' time, journeys by foot had to be planned along a route of public wells, such as the one in Nazareth.

Many wells in Jesus' time had capstones over them. Capstones keep the water much cleaner and also protect children from falling into the well. In addition, capstones provide a place to sit and a surface on which to work if one wants to transfer water from the drawing bucket into some other vessel.

In John 4, Jesus travels through Samaria and, tired from his journey, sits on the well. Often translators say "beside the well." But the Greek text says he sits "on" the well.

A woman approaches. The rules for a rabbi and any woman are clear in that society. Jesus is expected to move away, and the woman is expected to wait until he does so before she goes to draw her water. It is judged totally improper for a rabbi to talk to a woman in a public place, especially if she is unknown to him.

Worse yet, this is not any woman. She is a Samaritan woman who has had five husbands and now is living with a man to whom she is not married.

Amazingly, Jesus does not move, and the woman, needing water, approaches anyway. What follows is the longest conversation in all the Gospels, and one of the most marvelous.

Jesus opens the conversation by saying, "Give me a drink." At that time wells had no bucket suspended over them. Each traveler carried his own bucket. Jesus and the disciples certainly had such a bucket with them, but Jesus has allowed the disciples to take it with them into the local village. He deliberately puts himself in the position of needing the services of anyone who passes by.

Knowing that pious Jews would consider her bucket as unclean as herself, the woman responds: "How is it that you, a Jew, ask a drink of me, a woman of Samaria?"

Jesus surprises and confuses her by saying, "If you knew the gift of God, and who it is that is saying to you, 'Give me a drink,' you would have asked him, and he would have given you living water."

The woman is intrigued, but cautious: "Sir, you have no bucket, and the well is deep. Where do you get that living water? Are you greater than our ancestor Jacob, who gave us the well, and with his sons and his flocks drank from it?"

Then Jesus says: "Everyone who drinks of this water will be thirsty again, but those who drink of the water that I will give them will never be thirsty. The water that I will give will become in them a spring of water gushing up to eternal life."

And the woman, weary of her present life and routines, responds: "Sir, give me this water, so that I may never be thirsty."

As the conversation continues, Jesus amazingly reveals himself as the Messiah of God to this outcast woman. The woman says to him, "I know that Messiah is coming" (who is called Christ). "When he comes, he will proclaim all things to us." Jesus said to her, "I am he, the one who is speaking to you."

In that culture, Jews did not share common vessels with Samaritans, and rabbis did not have conversations with women. Thus, by asking this Samaritan woman for water, Jesus has granted her a special dignity, saying in effect, "I need you. Will you help me?" The place of women is dramatically elevated by this story, which thus serves the cause of justice. The woman becomes an evangelist and is sent back to her village, proclaiming a message of hope.

So, in one story we find the same four themes Jesus announced at the Nazareth synagogue: messiahship, proclamation, justice advocacy, and compassion.

NAZARETH: THE FLOWER OF GALILEE

In the fourth century, the ecclesiastic writer Jerome visits Nazareth and calls it "the flower of Galilee," perhaps for its beauty, perhaps because it lies at the center of a ring of rounded hills that resemble the petals of a rose.

2000 BC-100 BC
On the small hill where Nazareth was originally located, discovered artifacts date back to the third millennium BC. When the exiled tribes of Israel return from Egypt to the Promised Land, the hills of Nazareth become part of the tribe of Zebulon. In 922 BC, these hills are included with the Northern Kingdom in the schism that follows Solomon's death. For many centuries, ancient Nazareth remains humble and hidden. Because it is located off the main roads traveled by merchants and marauding armies, no mention of Nazareth is made until Jesus' arrival turns the town into a household name.

100 BC
Families from Judea settle Nazareth, laying the foundation for the town Jesus knew. From this time until the present, Nazareth is continuously populated.

6/5 BC
The angel Gabriel announces to Mary that she will bear a son, who is to be named Jesus.

3 BC-AD 30
Jesus spends childhood, youth, and most of his adult years at Nazareth.

Second Century
Relatives of Jesus continue to live in Nazareth. Likely they are descendants of Jude, whom the second-century writer Hegesippus calls the "brother of the Lord according to flesh" (see Mark 6:3). Much of our certainty about Nazareth as the home of the Holy Family is due to the memories they preserve.

Third Century
Jewish Christians build a church over the site of Mary's home.

Fourth Century
Emperor Constantine the Great protects and patronizes Christianity in the Roman Empire. This triggers a steady stream of pilgrims to the Holy Land.

100 BC | 1 | AD 100 | 200 | 300

ROMAN PERIOD

The Anonymous Pilgrim of Piancenza suggests that as late as 570 AD relationships in Nazareth are strained: "There are no women more beautiful throughout the entire country. They say their grace comes from Saint Mary, whom they claim as a relative. Though there is no love lost between Hebrews and Christians, these Hebrew women are actually kind."

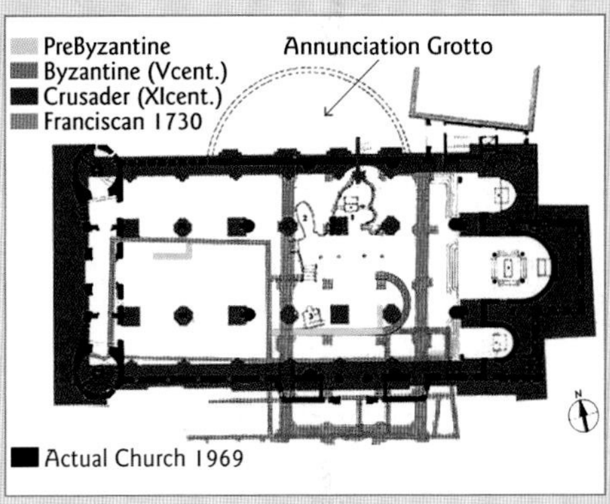

427
A Byzantine basilica (green, above) replaces the Jewish-Christian church over the home of Mary. The plan also shows the layout of the later Crusader church (red), Franciscan church (yellow), and the present day Church of the Annunciation (black).

614
The Persians invade Palestine, damaging many churches. After the Persians are defeated, the Byzantine Emperor Heraclius banishes the Jews of Nazareth (and likely the Jewish Christians as well) who have cooperated with the Persians. They are sent to exile in Egypt.

Left: The Crusades tremendously damage relations between East and West. A thousand years later, they still call for healing and reconciliation. So strong are these memories that they have become a campaign issue in modern Nazareth politics.

In the eleventh century, a Russian pilgrim mentions a round church dedicated to the Archangel Gabriel near the Nazareth spring also called Mary's Well. In 1750 Greek Orthodox monks rebuild the church, which remains standing today. Water flows from a crypt in the Church of St. Gabriel to a public well.

Twelfth Century
Tangred, the Norman Crusader, conquers Nazareth and rules as Prince of Galilee. Arab and Jew, Christian, and Muslim unite against the invaders. A large Crusader church is built to replace the Byzantine church.

In **1187** the Crusaders suffer a major defeat at the Horns of Hittin, a short distance east of Nazareth and near Tiberias.

On July 4, 1187, at the Horns of Hittin, the Crusaders are tricked by Salah al-Din into waging battle on an open plain during the height of summer. Overwhelmed by heat, heavy armor, and a shortage of water, they are soundly defeated, marking the beginning of the end for the Crusades.

Mameluke warrior.

1263

Nazareth is leveled on the orders of Sultan Bibars and his Mamelukes. The historian Abu el-Feda writes: "During a pause on Mount Tabor, a detachment of his army went to Nazareth by his order and destroyed the church of this city." Residents are ordered to adhere to Islam.

The Grotto of the Annunciation remains open to pilgrims, but no Christians are allowed to live in Nazareth until the Druze ruler Fakhr ed-Din revokes the decree in 1620.

Mt. Tabor rises from the outskirts of Nazareth. When Jesus talks about faith strong enough to move mountains, Mount Tabor—looking as if it were plunked down at random on an open plain—may have been his inspiration.

Pilgrims to Nazareth in search of Jesus sometimes find their greatest inspiration in the natural beauty of fields surrounding the town: "We preferred to look on the unchanged nature on which Jesus looked, and to wander among the flowers which had been pressed by his blessed feet. There was the wild thyme, and the stately hollyhock, and many a rock plant and meadow flower unknown in the flora of the Western world." —Reverend Andrew Thompson, Minister of Broughton Place Church, Edinburgh, Scotland, upon his visit to Nazareth in 1824

Nazareth, 1685. The House of the Holy Virgin lies just to the right of the large building at the far left of the engraving.

Time separates, place reconnects. Nazareth Village, located just 500 meters (540 yards) from the original site, has become the place where modern pilgrims can best visualize what the town would have been like in Jesus' day.

Fountain of the Virgin, 1855.

Nazareth in 1855, looking south toward the Plain of Esdraelon (Jezreel Valley), prophesied as Armageddon, where evil forces assemble, preparing for battle on the great day of God (Revelation 16:14-16; 20:8-9).

1620
Franciscans are permitted to locate in Nazareth. Initially, they see their mission as guarding the sacred ruins. This marks the beginning of Nazareth as we know it today. For the next three centuries, Christians who move to Nazareth from Syria and elsewhere live in harmony with their Muslim neighbors.

1730
The Franciscans build a small, unpretentious church over the Grotto of the Annunciation.

1799
Napoleon Bonaparte visits Nazareth and is disappointed by the simple, rustic shrine over the Grotto.

1500 | 1600 | 1700

OTTOMAN PERIOD

1861
The Edinburgh Medical Missionary Society founds Nazareth Hospital. Today it remains the oldest, continuously running hospital in all of Israel-Palestine.

1948
Israeli-Arab wars result in the current State of Israel. Nazareth's population explodes with Arab refugees.

1955
Father Bellarmino Bagatti conducts a major excavation of ancient Nazareth (below). Much of what is known about Nazareth's history from the time of Christ results from this work.

1960-69
A modern basilica is built over the Grotto of the Annunciation. Pope Paul VI makes a pilgrimage to observe the progress in 1964.

2000
Pope John Paul II visits Nazareth during millennium celebrations.

Nazareth Village opens to pilgrims.

2005
Former President Jimmy Carter and Swedish Prime Minister Carl Bildt (both Nobel Peace Prize recipients) visit Nazareth Village while in the Middle East to observe the Palestinian elections.

At Nazareth Village, the President and Prime Minister are treated to a first-century meal of bread, thyme, olive oil, cheese, and olives. Later, Carter writes in his Carter Center Web site that he was "truly amazed at (the village's) high quality and archaeological integrity."

Today
Nazareth is the political and administrative center of Galilee. It has the largest concentration of Christians in all the Holy Land.

Building continues at Nazareth Village as it re-creates the first-century farm and town that Jesus knew.

1800 1900 2000

BRITISH MANDATE STATE OF ISRAEL

NAZARETH VILLAGE: BUILT WITH LIVING STONES

Until the middle of the twentieth century, visitors to Nazareth can easily imagine the village Jesus called home.

But as the century enters its final decade, this idyllic town has been transformed into a teeming city of 70,000. Souvenir and falafel shops crowd the main boulevard. Horns blare from the cars and buses that jam the streets from dawn to dusk.

Pilgrims and visitors flock to Nazareth to see what Jesus saw and walk where Jesus walked but leave disappointed. Nazareth's residents regret that they cannot provide what guests to their beloved city long to experience.

And no one feels worse about this failure than Dr. Nakhle Bishara, a Christian, a ninth-generation Nazarene, and an Internist at the Nazareth Hospital.

Doctor Bishara, whose passion is history, can show pilgrims the dead stones from the few archaeological digs conducted in Nazareth. But he wants to be able to show them the living stones that would illuminate Jesus' teachings about love, compassion, and mercy.

Doctor Bishara desires this experience for those who come from abroad, and also for a new generation of local youth who can no longer observe, as he once did, the traditional farming practices and customs on which Jesus based his parables.

This is not simply an idle dream for Doctor Bishara. As he looks out the window of his hospital office, he can see a 40-dunam (10-acre) field, one of the last plots of undeveloped land in all Nazareth.

The land is owned by the Edinburgh Medical Missionary Society (now called EMMS Nazareth) of Scotland, which founded Nazareth Hospital in 1861. Because property values in Nazareth have soared, there is constant discussion about what to do with the plot. Develop parking? Use the land to help support the hospital? Or, as Doctor Bishara hopes, do something with a more lasting value? *(continued on page 73)*

In 1985, Dr. Nakhle Bishara begins to dream of a site where local youth and visitors from abroad can see the living stones of Jesus' teaching.

1984 | **1985** | **1986** | **1987**

Dr. Nakhle Bishara conceives project out of a concern that Arab Christians are losing the original cultural nuances of Jesus' teaching, and visitors to Nazareth don't

CARY SUMMERS

I have spent hundreds of hours walking the land of First Century Nazareth Village. Every hour provides new insights into God's word. There is a peace that transcends the surroundings and allows me to focus on the life and teachings of Jesus.

One of the greatest joys in being part of the Nazareth Village team is to see how profoundly the guest is impacted. They leave the village with new insights and understandings of how God used daily life to illustrate the depth of his word.

God has blessed Nazareth Village by bringing many diverse groups to see and hear Jesus' teachings, even during difficult times. This outpouring of God's grace continues to motivate me to be involved.

Before forming The Nehemiah Group, Cary served as an executive at Abercrombie and Fitch, Bass Pros Shops, and Silver Dollar City. The Nehemiah Group was engaged in 1998 to help determine the potential for this site. Cary continues to provide crucial consultation and direction as CEO of First Century Nazareth Village.

BADER MANSOUR

When I was a kid, we used to play soccer just a few yards away from the location where Nazareth Village is currently located. Those who watched the game would sit on top of what was later discovered to be an ancient winepress, one of the landmarks of the project!

For me, Nazareth Village is a refreshing stop in Nazareth, where many times we tend to get so busy with our own lives that we forget the most famous citizen of our city. It is a place where people from all around the world can come and learn more about the teachings of Jesus and meet local followers of him.

Bader, along with his brother Botrus, grew up in Nazareth. Today Bader works for a leading electronics firm and serves on the Nazareth Village Board.

Dr. Bishara frequently tells the story of the Prodigal Son to illustrate how the first-century meanings of Jesus' teachings have become buried over time (see pages 52-55). Art by Elizabeth Swindle

Reggie White (with Sherry Herschend), pastor and Hall of Fame football player, served as Honorary Trustee for Nazareth Village until his death in 2005.

1988 1989 1990 1991

Here at Nazareth Village, my dream was to show pilgrims the living stones of Jesus' legacy.
—Dr. Nakhle Bishara

RUTH GOODWIN-GROEN

Jesus' friend Peter wrote: "Although you have not seen him, you love him; and even though you do not see him now, you believe in him." (I Peter 1:8) My hope is that all who visit Nazareth Village will better understand the Jesus whom so many love and believe in.

LINDA FULLER

My husband, Millard, and I have dedicated our lives to expressing Christ's compassion by building affordable housing around the world. So I was thrilled when the call came to help rebuild the humble village Jesus called home.

Linda Fuller, Habitat for Humanity co-founder and member of Miracle of Nazareth International Foundation, shown here at the Sea of Galilee with David Link, Terry Troyer, and LeRoy Troyer.

REV. GLENN WITMER

In teaching settings with visiting Bible study groups, I often refer to the difficult creedal concept of Jesus being at once both fully human and fully divine. He is "divine" everywhere, but he was "fully human" here in this Land—especially in Nazareth, where he spent most of his life.

Seeing the re-created first-century village of Jesus' time gives us a fundamental understanding of how his Jewish upbringing, plus his family and village life as he grew up, provided much of the content for his teachings as an adult.

A tour experience in Nazareth Village, its Parable Walk, typical Roman-period homes and farm, and the only full reproduction of a synagogue of the period—all become part of the Fifth Gospel for us, showing so vividly who Jesus was and is. It becomes the context for the divine message he brought as a human who experienced life on earth along with us.

Glenn is the Israel liaison for his denomination and a lecturer on Biblical Archaeology and Geography of the Land for incoming tour groups.

DEAN DAVID T. LINK

Justice has been my life's calling, from a twenty-four-year stint as dean of University of Notre Dame Law School to being the founding Deputy Vice Chancellor and Provost of St. Augustine University College in South Africa. So it seemed only natural to join forces with those looking to create a setting in Nazareth dedicated to revealing the divine justice, mercy, and compassion of Jesus.

The Nazareth Village project has given me the opportunity to walk the very paths that Jesus walked. It has allowed me to help in spreading the good news.

David is the president and chief executive officer of the International Centre for Healing and the Law.

JOY JEANNINE (DAWSON) SVENSON

When my good friend Linda Fuller invited me to be part of a project to honor Jesus in his hometown, my mind raced with questions like, "Lord, do you really want me?"

But saying yes has taken me on an incredible journey with some of the most committed Christians I have known: Dr. Nakhle Bishara, Sherry Herschend, LeRoy Troyer, Michael Hostetler, George Khalil, and Botrus Mansour, to name only a few.

What a blessing it has been to walk my Nazareth Village walk. I pray that God will continue to bless the village and enable tens of thousands to also walk the Nazareth Village walk so they can experience our Lord and Savior Jesus Christ.

PRESIDENT JIMMY CARTER

While in the Middle East to observe Palestinian elections, I had a chance to visit Nazareth Village, a site that has been developed to emulate Nazareth and its rural surroundings during the time of Christ.

Beginning in 1996, Rosalynn and I supported a group of international and local Christians in acquiring the land and raising funds for the development of this ten-acre site, which lies inside the urban area of the city of Nazareth.

Given our respect for those involved, our expectations were lofty. Still, we were truly amazed at Nazareth Village's high quality and archaeological integrity.

1992

1993

WILMER MARTIN
My wife, Janet, and I believe that the life and teachings of Jesus of Nazareth, the Son of God, are needed in order to assist the world in finding peace, hope, and salvation. Nazareth Village welcomes people of all faiths and people of no faith to learn more about Jesus. Our prayer is that it will continue as a beacon of light in a dark world.

Wilmer and Janet Martin have developed the Friends of First Century Nazareth Village for individuals in Canada and the United States willing to donate annually to support Nazareth Village.

Among the miracles of Nazareth Village is the fact that representatives from traditional churches in the Middle East that date back to the time of Christ and more modern Evangelicals work together on the board and in the program—an almost unheard-of collaboration given the historic tensions between these two groups.

1994

• D. Michael Hostetler arrives in Nazareth to produce a video of a Good Samaritan story about an Arab taxi driver who saved the life of a severely wounded Jewish soldier by rushing him to the Nazareth Hospital.

• Doctor Bishara shares his vision for developing a visitor site illuminating the living stones of Jesus. Michael responds enthusiastically.

1995

• EMMS reacts positively to a presentation from Michael and Doctor Bishara and provides a generous grant as seed money.

• Michael recruits a band of volunteer consultants from the United States and the British Isles. They team with Christians from the Middle East to assess whether Doctor Bishara's dream is possible.

• The exploratory team's first decision is to adopt the Luke 4 passage of Jesus speaking at the synagogue in Nazareth as its scriptural cornerstone:

The Spirit of the Lord is upon me,
because he has anointed me
to bring good news to the poor.
He has sent me to proclaim release to the captives
and recovery of sight to the blind,
to let the oppressed go free,
to proclaim the year of the Lord's favor.

HUB ERICKSON
I went to Nazareth to help clear the hillside for the village and to see what this project was all about. I was matched up with Saleh Taha, a young Muslim who spoke a little English.

The work was dirty and hot, and Saleh would occasionally start a conversation with, "In Arabic there is an old saying from the Quran . . ." And I would come back with a saying from the New Testament. We became true friends and found we could discuss our differences openly.

Saleh showed me what Nazareth Village could really do: bring people together from all backgrounds and beliefs to learn more about the life, times, and teachings of Jesus of Nazareth. That's when I made my decision to get involved.

Hub spent most of his working life as chair and co-founder of Hall Erickson, Inc., a major producer of trade shows and expositions. But Hub, now in semiretirement, often calls Nazareth Village the real reason he was put on this earth. Hub's support for Nazareth Village was crucial to the project surviving its first years.

Queen Victoria shares wall space with Nazareth Village plans as the Edinburgh, Scotland, Medical Missionary Society (EMMS Nazareth) considers the proposal from the steering group.

1994

Dr. Bishara shares his vision with Michael Hostetler.

1995

Edinburgh (Scotland) Medical Missionary Society, which operates Nazareth Hospital and owns the desired land, grants seed money.

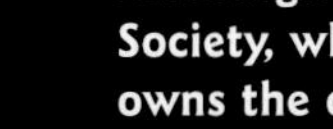

D. MICHAEL HOSTETLER

Jesus is both intensely personal and at the same time one of the most public figures in world history. Is it possible that by connecting with the human we come closer to the divine?

We began our work in Nazareth with the expectation that as we unpacked the world that Jesus knew, we could gain new insights on what he said. Our vision was to invite guests on a shared journey of discovery, together growing in our understanding of what it means to participate in a ministry that proclaims good news to the poor, brings justice and liberty for the captives, and demonstrates compassion by bringing sight to the blind.

Michael's journey of faith has taken him from Brazil to North America to Nazareth. He worked as a video and film producer and produced the feature film The Radicals *before launching Nazareth Village and serving as its first director.*

While church groups are not asked to officially endorse Nazareth Village, Dr. Nakhle Bishara and the Nazareth Village team consult closely with leaders throughout the Holy Land.

Tim Lichti leads devotions at the Mount of Beatitudes. The steering group spends much time visiting sites, reading Scripture, and praying as they seek God's will for the project.

1996

• Michael Hostetler, with the assistance of the Mennonite Board of Missions (now Mennonite Mission Network), moves with his wife, Virginia, and their two young children from the United States to Nazareth to lead the project.

• Michael forms a steering group of local and international members meeting two criteria:

1. Each has strong faith and walks daily with Jesus.
2. Each contributes something unique to the planning.

• To work at personal and cultural differences, they devote much time to reading Scripture and prayer. Doctor Bishara, named chair of the steering group, often reads the passage from Ephesians 4, reminding us that while we are all parts of the body, Jesus Christ is the head.

• Given the conflict between traditional Christians and modern Evangelicals in the Middle East, the steering group decides to operate the site as an independent not-for-profit (amuta, in Hebrew) project and not ask for official endorsements.

• While walking the land in December, Michael Hostetler, Joel Kauffmann, and archaeologist Stephen Pfann stumble onto a curious formation carved from the limestone bedrock. Pfann identifies it as a winepress.

1997

• A statement of purpose emerges from the steering group: *To create a visitor center and first-century village in the hometown of Jesus that illuminates his life and teaching to all peoples of the world.*

• Early thinking is to build a large visitor center filled with interactive displays and media presentations. Alongside this will be created a modest first-century village.

• The project is named Nazareth Village. The Nazareth Village symbol becomes a first-century lamp framed by a vaulted window, a reminder that Jesus came as a light in the darkness.

• The steering group establishes a set of principles to guide all aspects of the project:

1. To present a warm welcome and inviting spirit to visitors of all ages from around the world and of all ethnic origins, and to treat them as individuals on a spiritual pilgrimage (in other words, to treat people as Jesus would).
2. To incorporate an element of confession for the failure of Christians in the past, and to urge future tolerance and understanding among faith groups, especially the Christians, Jews, and Muslims of the Middle East.
3. To be a presence of healing and reconciliation that fulfills the spirit of Jesus and the long-standing precedent of the Nazareth Hospital.
4. To communicate the life and teachings of Jesus of Nazareth in a manner true to the biblical text and rooted in the best archaeological and anthropological expertise available.

• Guided by Stephen Pfann and the Center for the Study of Early Christianity, Jerusalem, workers carefully clear away weeds and centuries of accumulated rubble from the winepress. Pottery sherds confirm that the winepress existed in the Early Roman Period.

The implications of this discovery are enormous. Nazareth Village will not be building on an empty field. Instead, it will be building on a site of authentic agriculture predating Christ!

1996

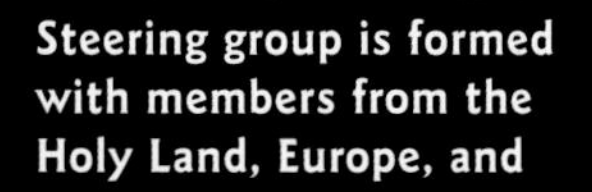

Steering group is formed with members from the Holy Land, Europe, and

Winepress carved into bedrock is discovered on the land.

1997

Archaeological dig confirms winepress was used and terraces farmed at the time of Jesus.

• The discoveries don't stop there. Workers find the bases of three watchtowers (above), quarries that likely contributed rock to the homes built in ancient Nazareth, and a rare irrigation conduit. Many crumbled terrace walls are confirmed as consistent with the building techniques of Jesus' time.

It is almost as if Jesus had stood on this very spot and dictated the parable that begins in Mark 12:1: *A man planted a vineyard, put a fence around it, dug a pit for the winepress, and built a watchtower*.

1998

• Encouraged by these discoveries, the steering group, in late January and after much prayer, votes unanimously to move from exploration to building.

After the decision, the members of the steering group walk out to the land. Each places a rock on a pile to symbolize the living stones of Jesus Christ.

• The steering group divides into two boards. The Nazareth Village Board will oversee the development and building of Nazareth Village.

• The Miracle of Nazareth International Foundation (MNIF) will work to raise the resources necessary for the project. They choose the word "miracle" out of recognition that it will require the hand of God to raise the needed support for such a complex project fraught with such great obstacles.

• MNIF agrees to fund the initial building and infrastructure at Nazareth Village, knowing that this ambitious goal will challenge their business skills and faith.

• Hundreds of volunteers—children, men, women, traditional Christians, Evangelicals, Muslims—show up at the hillside below Nazareth Hospital to clear the land on which

The work of the Nazareth Village Board (top) is supported by the Miracle of Nazareth International Foundation (above).

Nazareth Village will be built, despite the fact that volunteering is not a common practice in the Holy Land.

• As the ancient terrace walls are restored, the contours of the hillside begin to take the form that would have been familiar to Nazareth's most famous resident: Jesus.

• Bolstered by the ongoing archaeological discoveries and research, building plans shift to downsize the visitor center and focus instead on a full-scale first-century village and farm.

1999

• By March, the first home (funded in part by a Nazareth women's group) is completed and another underway.

• Even though opening is scheduled for 2000, there is no sense of panic. Since construction

Volunteers clean the winepress and clear the land.

of the homes is being done in a first-century style by workers dressed in the clothing of Jesus' time, the building process can continue past opening as part of the attraction.

• Olive trees from groves being cleared for building in other parts of the Holy Land, including 27 from a school in Nazareth, are replanted at Nazareth Village. Some of these trees are hundreds of years old and arrive looking like little more than shriveled stumps.

But the ability of olive trees to regenerate is one of the world's great miracles. As these ancient trees take root and begin to sprout, they become a fitting metaphor for the project.

• A portion of the YMCA building that sits at the foot of the Nazareth Village land is rented to the project. The top floor is gutted and fitted with offices, a gift shop, and a series of simple displays that will set the stage for a visit to the first-century farm and village.

• A connecting bridge is built from the YMCA to the hillside. It allows visitors to leave the modern world behind and enter the time of Christ.

1998

Steering group commits to move forward from planning to building Nazareth Village as a not-for-profit (amuta) project.

Nazareth Village Board and Miracle of Nazareth International Foundation are formed to direct construction, program development, and fundraising.

Hundreds of volunteers clear the land.

1999

Original terraces are reconstructed.

Initial first-century home is built.

Centuries-old olive trees are moved to land.

FRED AITKEN

My first encounter with Nazareth Village was in 1995, when Mike Hostetler came to the Edinburgh Medical Missionary Society to present his vision for Nazareth Village. EMMS owned Nazareth Hospital and adjacent land, a part of which was considered an ideal location for the village. Contrary to the expectations of the Scottish board, Mike did not give a hard sell and plainly said he didn't know when asked a question he couldn't answer. This was greatly in his favour. The board endorsed the vision and donated the £30,000 ($50,000) Mike asked for to explore the idea.

EMMS appointed Fred Holmes and me as their representatives on the steering group, and the next few years proved unique and thrilling. From quite different backgrounds and traditions, we on the steering group experienced a unity of vision and quality of fellowship that seldom happens in the ordinary path of life.

And so, Nazareth Village was born and the vision became a reality. Our doors opened to the world, and in the village's short life to date, pilgrims and visitors have indeed come from all corners of the earth and have been deeply moved by the experience.

Fred Aitken (center), in Rumbling Bridge, Scotland, with LeRoy (left) and Terry Troyer (right) of The Troyer Group.

LEROY TROYER

In 1984, my wife, Phyllis, and I were on a Middle Eastern tour. As our bus approached Nazareth, the guide said, "There really is nothing to see here." I said to him, "There must be something in Jesus' hometown about his life. Isn't there even a carpenter shop?" To my dismay, the bus just drove through the town. As someone who has dedicated his life to architectural design and building, I was extremely disappointed.

This memory came back eleven years later, when Dale Schumm contacted me to discuss the idea of building a visitor center in Nazareth. I quickly agreed to go to Nazareth with my son, Terry, and a team of others to explore the possibilities.

What an incredible moment of faith. Here I was, a farm boy and graduate of Notre Dame University, suddenly using both of these backgrounds to create a conceptual rendering of the first-century farm and village Jesus knew.

With Nazareth Village now up and running, I take great satisfaction in knowing that Nazareth now has a carpenter shop, and buses filled with pilgrims don't pass through Nazareth. Instead, they consider it a prime destination.

LeRoy is the Founder/President of The Troyer Group, Inc., an architectural/engineering firm located in Mishawaka, Indiana. The Troyer Group specializes in health care, senior living, college and university work as well as civil engineering.

2000 and Beyond

• After several successful trial runs with test groups, Nazareth Village finally opens in September, the Year of Our Lord 2000. Buses bearing visitors from around the world pull up to the gates.

For the first time, pilgrims to Nazareth are able to do as Doctor Bishara once dreamed. They can see what Jesus saw in the town he called home, walk where Jesus walked, and experience his remarkable words of love, compassion, and mercy with the eager ears of a first-century citizen. *(continued on page 78)*

An early concept drawing of Nazareth Village. The plan shifts dramatically with the discovery that this land is an actual first-century farm.

RIYAD HADDAD

The study I went through to design a first-century Galilean village made me understand more about architecture and, at the same time, who Jesus is. I had to imagine myself there. I benefited as an architect in ways I had not anticipated. More important, my appreciation for Jesus grew in a way I had not expected.

As we began construction, we knew we were not just building homes; we were also building relationships. I imagine this is what Jesus and Joseph already knew as they built homes in Nazareth 2000 years ago.

Nazareth architect Riyad Haddad, pictured here with North American architect LeRoy Troyer. Riyad and LeRoy form a cross-Atlantic partnership that symbolizes the challenges and successes of Nazareth Village.

2000

Nazareth Village is opened in September.

2001

Additional homes are constructed, using first-century techniques and

SHERRY HERSCHEND

Pat Boone planted a seed in my heart many years ago when he shared his vision for creating a place that feels like one is visiting Jesus' hometown. In 1998 I asked Cary Summers to go to Israel and investigate the proposed Nazareth Village project and answer two questions:

Is this a God-sized/inspired project?

Is it truly of eternal significance?

Cary's response to me was so overwhelmingly positive that I accepted a nomination to serve on the board. And I asked Cary to help see this vision to completion.

Then I learned that the project was underfunded and in danger of being canceled. According to Genesis 12, we are blessed to be a blessing. Using this as a measuring stick, I realized that my purpose and giftedness in this project could be to act as an encourager and to help fund it.

In return, I have been blessed to truly discover God's ultimate mission for my life (Matthew 28:19). I was called by God to serve on a project that is changing lives for eternity by showing generations to come the teachings of Jesus—on the very farmland and paths where he walked.

And I have been blessed to be part of a team with similar commitment. When God wants to accomplish a task, he will most always impress several people with a common vision and purpose.

I am excited that this book will preserve the origins of First Century Nazareth Village so that history will not be lost, and the world that follows will always know how God brought so many people from so many places together to re-create the Nazareth that Jesus knew.

Sherry is co-owner/co-founder of Herschend Family Entertainment, which owns and/or operates a series of attractions throughout North America, including Silver Dollar City, Missouri; Dollywood, Tennessee; and Stone Mountain, Georgia.

TIM LICHTI

My experience with Nazareth Village gave me a sense of what is possible in joining hands across religious boundaries. The realization that God was in our midst helped me sense the awe that others would experience when visiting this land.

The role of Nazareth Village in building foundation blocks toward peace in the region still inspires me. I am pleased to hear the stories of groups from different backgrounds exploring the village together. Jesus still has the ability to bring healing into the most difficult of circumstances.

I will always treasure the friendships during late-night meals or engaging the local shopkeepers. And I'll value the memories of strolls through the winding streets of Nazareth, walking where Jesus walked. Even if the steps may not have been in the same footpath, the desire to find spiritual oneness with Jesus increased with every stride.

Tim is former director of Menno-Hof, a Mennonite-Amish visitor center in Shipshewana, Indiana, that provided much of the inspiration for Nazareth Village. Currently he serves as a regional minister for his denomination.

Members of the exploratory team pose with Nazareth Mayor Rames Jarrisi (red vest).

Original Exploratory Team

Elia Abdo
Fred Aitken
Dr. Nakhle Bishara
Riyad Haddad
Dr. Fred Holmes
D. Michael Hostetler
Joel Kauffmann
George Khalil
Tim Lichti
Botrus Mansour
LeRoy Troyer
Terry Troyer
Ronald E. Yoder

Honorary Trustees

President Jimmy Carter and Rosalynn Carter
Reverend Theodore M. Hesburgh, C.S.C., President Emeritus, University of Notre Dame

Nazareth Village Board Members

Fred Aitken*
Robin Arnott
Rev. Dr. Naim Ateek
Najed Azzam
Dr. Nakhle Bishara*
Ihab Elimi
Ruth P. Goodwin-Groen
Dr. Fred Holmes*
George Khalil*
Violet Khoury*
Chow Leng Wee
Tim Lichti*
Bader Mansour
Botrus Mansour*
Dr. Imad N. Shehadeh
Glenn Witmer
John Woodhead
Ronald E. Yoder*

Miracle of Nazareth International Foundation Board of Trustees

Pat Boone*
Dr. Gary Cook*
Hub Erickson*
Arthur C. Frantzreb*
Linda Fuller*
Harry M. Hargrave
Sherry Herschend*
David T. Link*
Wilmer Martin
Allen Mathis Jr.*
Ronald A. Mulder
Dr. Dale Schumm*
Nelson L. Showalter, RPh
Joy Jeannine (Dawson) Svenson*
LeRoy Troyer*

* Board members when Nazareth Village opened in 2000

2002

First-century synagogue is built.

2003

GEORGE KHALIL
When I heard of Nazareth Village from Michael Hostetler and met with Doctor Bishara, their vision inspired me. When they invited me to join an advisory group, I immediately said yes.

What do I see from Nazareth Village that is helpful to the community? My own ministry (Emmaus Bible School) reaches out to youth and children with the gospel (forty-five percent of the Arab population is under the age of nineteen). I saw the potential through Nazareth Village to reach these same groups. So I put my weight behind this to invite schools to visit the village.

Where have we come? Along with international visitors, thousands of youth and children visit Nazareth Village each year, and feedback from schools is tremendous encouragement for us to continue. In fact, many of these children now volunteer as villagers.

George Khalil, original member of the Nazareth Village Board, works as administrator of Emmaus Bible School and as a Nazareth carpenter, both occupations that help him identify with Jesus.

Today, over 10,000 students a year from Israel-Palestine schools visit Nazareth Village. On some occasions, Jewish and Arab groups plan trips together to promote greater understanding.

MAHA SAYEG
Two thousand years ago, Nazarenes kicked Jesus out of Nazareth. Two thousand years later, I as a local Nazarene wanted to be a part of bringing him back to Nazareth and to witness to the world about Jesus today.

Maha serves on the staff for Nazareth Village and has been part of the project from its earliest days.

The Nazareth Jesus Knew author **JOEL KAUFFMANN** (left) and designer **MERRILL MILLER** (below). Joel served as part of the original planning group for Nazareth Village. He also developed the Parable Walk and visitor center displays. Merrill designed the Nazareth Village logo and helped create and build the visitor center displays.

2000 and Beyond *(continued)*

• In the years since opening, a synagogue, an olive press, a sheep pen, and more homes have been added.

The excitement of growth is often countered by times of difficulty when political tensions make tourism difficult. Perhaps this is fitting, for Jesus lived during dangerous and uncertain times. That made his call for peace and reconciliation all the more profound.

But through the ups and the downs, the celebrations and the uncertainties, Nazareth Village and the many people who have provided their time, talents, and resources to make it possible remain committed to carrying on its singular, life-changing vision:

Creating a living presentation of the life, time, and teachings of Jesus of Nazareth for all the world.

CHOW LENG WEE
What captured my attention, and subsequently my involvement, was the amount of research, prayer, and planning that went into making Nazareth Village a place for people to reflect on the life of Jesus. The project did not just take a tourist approach but instead was also meant for Bible believers who want to have a deeper understanding of this little town where Jesus began his ministry.

HARRY HARGRAVE
I became involved with Nazareth Village via the enthusiasm of my father-in-law Allen Mathis Jr (an original MNIF board member). It has been a rewarding experience to see the physical growth of the facility and the impact it has had on Nazareth. It also serves as a vivid example of the bridge between different faiths in this region, which links the historical perspectives of Christians, Jews, and Muslims.

Nazareth Village mourns the loss but celebrates the contribution of three of its most valued team members, who died before the publication of this book: **ALLEN MATHIS JR.** (above) gave generously, along with Hub Erickson, to match Sherry Herschend's gift that allowed us to build and open the first phase of the project. **DR. DALE SCHUMM** (below left) was invaluable in laying the groundwork for the project. **MARK GOODMAN**, an Architectural Conservator, (below right) oversaw the village transition from blueprints to brick and mortar.

2004
Olive press is completed.

2005

President Carter visits.

Contractor Karam Hawa, a specialist in first-century construction methods, offered to have his company work for as long as a year without pay to finish the synagogue when Nazareth Village ran short of funds.

RONALD E. YODER

The significance of Nazareth Village is the illumination of the life and teachings of Jesus where he grew up, in a modern context of religious, political, and ethnic strife where the vast majority of persons still do not embrace the reconciling message of Jesus more than two thousand years later.

Ron spent many years working with the media and international ministries of his denomination. Today he serves as President/CEO of Virginia Mennonite Retirement Community in Harrisonburg, Virginia.

DR. FRED HOLMES

In 1995 the whole Western world was striving to find an appropriate way to celebrate the new millennium. But there was barely any mention of the reason for the millennium: that it was two thousand years from the birth of Jesus of Nazareth.

What fired my interest in Nazareth Village was the thought that there should be some permanent recognition of this fact in Jesus' hometown. It would be a witness of his uniqueness to the whole world so that in this new millennium people could still take seriously the birth, life, death, and teachings of Jesus, and the need to live our lives in conformity to Jesus.

Doctor Holmes served as a surgeon at Nazareth Hospital, as a board member for both EMMS Nazareth and Nazareth Village, and has led many tours in the Holy Land.

Nazareth Village quickly captures the attention of the world media. Reporters and camera crews from CNN, the BBC, *The [London] Times*, German Wire Services, Associated Press, *USA Today*, *Biblical Archaeology Review*, and *Christianity Today* are just a few of the international media to produce articles and media specials on the life of Jesus.

Alan Rabinowitz, a Jewish writer for Israel's national newspaper, *The Jerusalem Post*, calls Nazareth Village "a unique religious-cultural intersection" between Jews, Muslims, and Christians. He observes: "It struck me that the meticulous effort . . . to replicate these ancient walls might in some small way help dismantle some modern ones."

BOTRUS MANSOUR

Jesus of Nazareth brought together individuals, both local and international, from the worldwide church in a joint effort to glorify his name in his own hometown. The Lord's hand was obvious from the beginning, and he led the way in overcoming many different obstacles.

Nazareth Village has become an oasis for meditating on Jesus' teaching in the midst of the desert of daily life in Nazareth. Through telling the parables of Jesus in the environment where they were originally taught, we gain a new and fresh understanding.

The spirit a visitor to Nazareth Village will experience is that of the kindness and love reflected in Jesus' teachings. I thank the Lord that he gave me the privilege to serve him and contribute to the founding of this special place.

Botrus (Peter, in English) is a lawyer, the director of the Baptist School in Nazareth, and founding member of the Nazareth Village Board. When board members argued, they would remind themselves that Peter and the disciples also had disagreements.

STEPHEN PFANN

With Nazareth Village, we have a piece of property that is nearly contiguous with the original town, and it just happens by chance or by miracle that it has not been developed, because everything else in the modern city of Nazareth has been dug up or covered by concrete.

The village and surrounding farm serve as a living laboratory on the life and teachings of Jesus. As people come in increasing numbers, it will also provide work and revenue for the people of Nazareth.

Nazareth Village has widespread appeal because it is essentially a Jewish village from biblical times in a modern Arab town, and it is most meaningful to Christians.

Prof. Pfann is President of the University of the Holy Land, Jerusalem.

How is First Century Nazareth Village supported?

Nazareth Village operates as a not-for-profit organization. Our goal is to support daily operations through entrance fees and gift-shop sales.

An international network of friends assists with the development of new construction. When regional conflicts reduce the flow of visitors, additional contributions are sometimes needed to help offset temporary loss of income.

What will I experience at Nazareth Village?

Nazareth Village is a first-century farm and village located next to the Nazareth Hospital, a half kilometer (one-third mile) from the center of the Old City in Nazareth, Israel.

Guests encounter hillside farm terraces growing olive trees, grape arbors, and other crops typical of Jesus' day. Donkeys, goats, and a flock of sheep roam the land. Visits continue in a fully reconstructed village that includes homes, shops, a synagogue, and a working olive press.

Villagers in first-century costumes demonstrate the farm practices and daily life Jesus knew. Tours take about an hour and a half. Special-event meals and programs are available upon request.

To arrange a visit or learn how you can help support Nazareth Village, please contact

Nazareth Village
P.O. Box 2066
Nazareth 16100 Israel

Phone: 972-4-645-6042
or 972-4-655-9301

Fax: 972-4-655-9295

E-mail: info@nazarethvillage.com

Web: www.nazarethvillage.com

When calling internationally, dial your country's international access code (011 from the USA or Canada) before the listed number.

Nowhere are the living stones of Jesus' legacy more visible than in the hardworking staff at Nazareth Village, who willingly go a second mile/kilometer to make your visit memorable.

Gift Shop: Nazareth Village offers an online Gift Shop, where you can purchase a unique selection of handcrafted art from the Holy Land, first-century costumes, custom-designed Christmas cards, pottery, jewelry, spices, and additional copies of this book! Items will be shipped directly to you. Check www.nazarethvillage.com/gshop/

Contributions to Nazareth Village may be made at our Israel address or at

(USA)
Miracle of Nazareth International Foundation
550 Union Street, Mishawaka, IN 46544, USA
E-mail: NehemiahGr@aol.com
Phone: 574-259-9976

(Canada)
Nazareth Village, Mennonite Church Canada
600 Shaftesbury Blvd.
Winnipeg, MB R3P 0M4, Canada

To learn more about EMMS Nazareth and Nazareth Hospital, log online at www.nazarethhospital.org or www.emms.org